Re-solving the Economic Puzzle

To Erlyne & Len —
with thanks for
your friendship
& with hopes for
a changed economy.

Walt &
Editor-in-love Erika

Re-solving the Economic Puzzle

Walter Rybeck

SHEPHEARD-WALWYN (PUBLISHERS) LTD

First published in 2011 by
Shepheard-Walwyn (Publishers) Ltd
107 Parkway House, Sheen Lane,
London SW14 8LS
www.shepheard-walwyn.co.uk and
www.ethicaleconomics.org.uk

British Library Cataloguing in Publication Data
A catalogue record of this book
is available from the British Library

ISBN: 978-0-85683-281-9

To contact the author: waltrybeck@aol.com

Typeset by Alacrity,
Winscombe, Somerset, UK
Printed in the USA
by Edwards Brothers Inc

To Buddy, Ry, Art, Erika,
Rick and Alex
who in their various ways
made – and make –
our world more civil,
more culturally rich,
more equitable

Endorsements of the book

William J. Byron, Professor of Business & Society, St. Joseph's University, former president, Catholic University of America: Commitment and competence characterize Rybeck's life-long effort to promote the common good through creative application of land taxation policies. This book revives the insights of Henry George and reveals the difference one man can make in the struggle to promote economic justice and prosperity, if only policy makers will listen.

Former Pittsburgh Congressman William J. Coyne: Our city pioneered in gradually shifting property taxes off buildings onto land values. This modest use of a land tax helped make Pittsburgh's renewal a model for the nation. The full-blown use of this tool that Rybeck urges could go far to restore our nation's economic health.

Ken Hechler, formerly White House assistant, Congressman, and West Virginia Secretary of State: This book re-tells the story of how coal, oil and timber became a curse to Appalachia because these resources attracted exploiters who left the bulk of mountain people in poverty. Rybeck, a native West Virginian, offers a workable formula that will make our natural riches a blessing for the population as a whole.

Stephen R. Reed, Harrisburg Mayor, 1982-2010: Rybeck shows how an innovative real estate tax policy stimulates economic growth and job creation. We know it works. It turned Pennsylvania's Capital City from the nation's second most distressed city into a nationally recognized economic development success story.

Contents

Acknowledgements

READERS WILL RECOGNIZE that the central theme of this book borrows heavily from common knowledge and from the wisdom of the ages as passed down by writers, philosophers, theologians and statesmen, living and dead. Most are unnamed but I am in their debt.

Far from anonymous were those who critiqued early drafts. My wife Erika was my sounding board, constant timekeeper and stand-in for readers without economics training. My sons Rick and Alex offered thoughtful corrections and additions. Nephew Ted Rybeck and cousins Norman Suslock and Robert Treuer provided invaluable help. Others with incisive comments were John Rybicki, Mason Gaffney, Vivianne and Elliot Pierce, Robert Rochlin, Tom Carcaterra, Robert Calvert, Won Yin and Anne Southard.

Among those who sparked important insights in recent years have been Alanna Hartzok, co-director of the Earth Rights Institute, Father William Byron, former president of Catholic University of America (now Professor of Business and Society at St. Joseph's University), Steven Cord, instigator of land taxes in many Pennsylvania cities, Nadine Stoner, head of the Wisconsin Property Owners League and editor of *GroundSwell,* Joshua Vincent, director of the Center for the Study of Economics, Edward Dodson, head of the School of Cooperative Individualism, Mike Curtis of the Arden land tax enclave, city planner Chuck Metalitz, Lindy Davies, director of the Henry George Institute, Peoria stockbroker and biblical scholar John Kelly, John Fisher of the Canadian Green Party, Scottish ecologist and land reformer Shirley-Ann Hardy, and journalist-economist Fred Harrison of England. Also stimulators of thoughtful inquiry have been Pat Aller, William Batt, Margaret Bell, Polly Cleveland, George Collins, Father Francis Gargani, Elizabeth Gordon, Ruth Gruenberg, William B. Irvine, Harry Pollard, Heather Ramoff, Carl Shaw, Mark Sullivan, Professor Nicolaus Tideman and Margaret Locke Newhouse.

To brainstorm the first draft, Ted and my sons arranged a family reunion-seminar weekend with serious reviews by adults and youngsters, with creative slogans, bumper stickers, public service announcements and jingles about land justice for comic relief. Attending Rybecks and in-laws not listed above were Chick, Jan, Naomi, Gabe, Shoshana, Abe, Blanche, Ry, Mia, Emma, Ellen Czaplewski, Ellen Brodsky, Vivian and Mark Brodsky, Judy Krivit, John and Vicky Czaplewsky and Liz Welniak. Treuers not listed above were Paul, Mary, Derek, Elissa, Zoe and Adrienne Marks.

Helping to keep me from taking the work too seriously was scientist friend Joseph Sucher, whose cynical response to the book's basic formula was a classic: "Nobody will adopt it – it makes too much sense!"

I owe special thanks to an admired mentor, Lowell Harriss, chairman emeritus of the Columbia University economics department. We participated in an intensive study of U.S. assessment practices and served together on the Schalkenbach Foundation board. Touchingly, a few months before his death, at age 97, he sent detailed handwritten suggestions about my draft and phoned to say it was urgent "to get the message out".

Public Management (PM) magazine used an article titled "Retooling Property Taxes" as the lead piece in the magazine's March 2010 issue, which is published by the International City/County Management Association (ICMA), Washington, D.C. The article was based on successful United States land tax reforms detailed in Chapter 28. The magazine article elicited follow-ups from a number of local government managers. My thanks to *PM* editor Beth Payne.

It was my good fortune that Shepheard-Walwyn in London, England, took my manuscript under its wings. Publisher Anthony Werner, along with editor Alice Aldous and designer Jean Desebrock, combined great care and remarkable speed to enable this book to become part of the search for new economic directions. They fully shared the author's eagerness that messages herein would contribute useful guidance to policymakers working to halt the current crisis and to avert future ones.

The usual caveat, as true as it is necessary, is that none of the many who tried to help with the book are to blame for errors of fact or concept, for which the author bears full responsibility.

Introduction

THIS BOOK BRINGS good news to those who want an America with full employment, a sustainable prosperity without roller-coaster ups and downs, and a return to constructive political and social discourse without rancor.

This is not to deny our critical problems. In this richest nation the world has ever known, from New Orleans to Detroit, from Boston to Los Angeles, in grand cities like Chicago and New York and in rural areas from Appalachia to the Ozarks, people are mired in poverty. Families and babies go hungry despite our prodigious ability to produce food and despite the mountains of wasted food. Large numbers of willing workers find no job in the face of unmet social and individual needs. Hordes of homeless city people roam the streets side by side with boarded-up housing. The bad news is that, if we allow current trends to continue, the outlook for our future is dismal.

However, waiting in the wings is a way to change course and revive what has been the genius of our economic and cultural life. This change requires a reform that is fully consistent with American traditions and ideals. In fact it harks back to one of the most significant factors undergirding our nation's remarkable earlier success – a factor that somehow has been all but obliterated from our collective memory. As will be seen, it involves removing an injustice that is corroding the enterprise system and that is increasingly making us more akin to nations characterized by sharp divisions between the underprivileged and overprivileged.

Many people are angry with the poor, the hungry, the homeless and the unemployed. "I made it on my own, so why can't they?" they ask, perhaps forgetting those who gave them a lift along the way. If the victims are at fault, there is no need to question whether there may be legitimate reasons that they are not "making it". A majority, however, tend to sympathize with the misery of their fellow citizens, leading them to support private charities and public assistance programs. Yet neither camp – those with empathy and those without – seem inclined to pursue the root causes of our socio-economic ills.

Only those who are Pollyannaish can say all is well with our nation when jails and prisons are overflowing and when mental illness is rampant. These are wake-up calls reminding us to understand and confront our festering social malignancies.

Another Injustice to Conquer

A serious injustice permeates our country. Laws allow individuals to appropriate values created by other people's work, depriving those who created these values of a fair return. This "legalized theft" sets off a chain reaction that has been a factor in the nation's repetitive boom and bust cycles. It blocks job creation. It eats away at our enterprise system. It infects our democratic institutions. It diminishes social unity and harmony.

The distress following the latest economic meltdown – all the lost jobs, lost homes, lost savings, lost businesses – underscores the need for systemic reform. Only by confronting the underlying economic distortion infecting our system can our nation live up to its lofty ideals and its promise to its own people and to the world at large.

Struggles against great injustice are proud chapters of our history. The ethnic cleansing of Native Americans and the enslavement of kidnapped Africans in our nation's formative years shock 21st century sensibilities. Women's voices as voters were not recognized until the 1920s. It seems almost incomprehensible now that these evils were once so widely accepted. Having overcome past injustices entitles us to have a high degree of confidence that the flaws cited in these pages can be corrected as well. Each effort to correct and atone for a serious departure from our professed aims bring us closer to a society that practices as well as preaches that *all* men and *all* women are endowed with equal rights.

Deviations from our goal of justice do not contradict the fact that America has been and remains a remarkable society and a splendid ideal. History teaches us not to be stunned that decent citizens and brilliant leaders can be blind to monumental injustices. The injustice described in this book is widely practiced and accepted by good people. No irony intended. We honor Washington, Jefferson, and other Founding Fathers for their vision and political genius despite their having been slave owners. By the same token, perpetrators of our current injustice should not be held culpable. We should condemn the *injustice itself*, not the decent people who are actively or passively caught up in it with little awareness that they are doing so.

Americans are frequently told that our country is the greatest, the best hope of mankind, and the like, persuading some that our nation is close to perfection. To them, asserting that the nation is contaminated with a serious flaw may be so jarring that naming this flaw may invite instant disbelief and a disinclination to listen further. Of course, people who profit from an injustice tend to like and defend it, even to the extent of calling reform efforts unpatriotic. They need to be reminded that correcting the nation's failings is among the most fundamental expressions of liberty for which patriots have sacrificed their lives and fortunes.

That said, I can identify with those who find it hard to consider that a long-standing feature of our economy, one that is embedded in our legal system, is poisoning our society. The prevalent economic theories offered in college courses make it difficult to visualize the problem or to imagine that, in some essential respects, America is not on the right path. My initial reaction to a contrary view was to deny it.

To Demonstrate an Injustice

Mainstream economists pride themselves on being analytical and non-judgmental. A message of this book is that without *ethical* inquiry there can be little understanding of our Great Recession or how to alleviate our chronic economic failures.

Imagine that slavery still existed. Consider how today's social scientists would confront it. They would devise elaborate computer models to project what would happen if the institution were expanded or diminished. They would construct sophisticated regression analyses to test how various policy options would affect slaves, slave owners, and those who were neither slaves nor owners. They would measure the impacts on different industries and types of agriculture. They would indicate whether winners or losers would predominate. Mathematical formulas and input-output models, along with precise indications of margins of error, would give their findings an aura of scientific certainty. Their learned articles on the topic would reveal their discovery that slavery is not a single problem, that it is actually a multiplicity of problems, and (to ensure that their continued studies are adequately funded) that each of these facets of the problem require considerable additional research.

No need to pursue this illustration further. Econometric manipulation of data would throw little light on the central question: *Was the institution of slavery right or wrong?* Ethical tests are needed. This requires holding social practices up for scrutiny to see whether they conform to the highest moral codes of the people and of the nation. Slavery represented a disconnect from these high codes. A burden of this book is to show that a similar serious disconnect exists with respect to certain land and taxation policies. To make such a case, reference to concepts of fairness, logic, history and bedrock American ideals will be relied upon, however old-fashioned this approach may appear in contrast to elegant algebraic formulations.

This is not to denigrate the potent and highly useful tools of modern economists. These tools can verify the effects of various reforms and programs that are contemplated or already implemented. It is no criticism of these tools to note that they do not answer the initial question of whether something is morally acceptable. Fortunately, as it turns out, experience tells us that doing the right thing usually produces the greatest benefits for the greatest numbers.

Road Map of the Book

Part I at the very outset spells out the nature of the injustice that is undermining our economy. It is followed by a "secret remedy", so called because it has been kept out of the public eye for a long time. Then a chapter on land and property rights aims to clarify the problem and ways of dealing with it.

Part II tells how I accidentally became alerted to the land issue.

Part III traces people and events that, in the fullness of time, provided a framework for helping me confront critical land issues. Sharing these intellectual journeys may enable others to more readily understand, if not accept, the conclusions I have reached. Of course, life embraces much more than economics and I recount my good fortune in being exposed to a rich cafeteria of opportunities. Asking why too many Americans are denied entry to such opportunities brings us back full circle to economic inequities and explains much of the motivation for writing this book.

Part IV tells of a remarkable cast of mentors and co-workers who inspired me and wove a common thread of insights into land issues throughout my careers in journalism, politics, and economics.

Part V recounts neglected or glossed over aspects of American history that have a surprising bearing on current problems and that point to forgotten conditions and policies that practically cry out for revival.

Part VI describes successful applications of the tax strategies discussed throughout the book. One chapter addresses successes in the United States, another cites some overseas successes, and the final chapter in this part deals with the special case of natural resources, contrasting ruinous approaches in Appalachia with more equitable approaches in Alaska.

Part VII specifies how land policy changes can deal constructively with a broad range of seemingly intransigent problems and help attain the more equitable and prosperous America that we all yearn for.

PART 1

ANOTHER CRACK
IN THE
LIBERTY BELL

THIS BOOK IS WRITTEN in the firm belief that Niccolo Machiavelli, astute politician and observer of human nature as he was, mistakenly used the word "never" when he wrote: *"People are always provoked by small injustices but never by great injustices."*

1

Problems Hidden in Full Sunlight

"NOBODY SAW IT COMING."

High officials, leading economists, pundits, bankers, legislators, and fiscal regulators insistently repeated that phrase after the 21st century's initial boom turned into an ugly bust. They were not paying attention, nor were they studying history.

Land economists, a rare breed, knew it was coming. Since the early 1800s, Americans have experienced economic breakdowns almost every generation. Most were relatively mild while some were catastrophic. They happened mostly for the same underlying reason. Speculative landholding sprees fueled the start of each cycle. Substantial numbers of individuals and businesses that had engaged in production diverted their efforts to the non-productive pursuit of profits from runaway land costs. When inflated land rents and land prices exceeded a great many people's and firms' ability to pay, the bubble burst, wiping out jobs, enterprises, and the savings of the mass of people who were behaving prudently.

Each panic, depression, and recession whittled away a bit more of Americans' optimism, pride in workmanship, and trust in the nation's economic and political systems. Each time, another bit of liberty was eroded.

Underneath All, the Land

Whether the economy rises or falters, whether it is erratic or on a steady course, is closely related to how land is treated. Land is so

3

critical because it is the source of all wealth. Land and the natural resources on or in it are the elementary building blocks of every economy. Land provides all the basic essentials for human survival. How we treat land touches nearly every aspect of the economy – from our homes to the health of cities, from family farms to giant manufacturing plants, from availability of jobs to the profitability of firms. Economic troubles arise when land monopoly deprives large segments of society of their access to the gifts of nature.

Land monopoly? In America? Most people are astounded to learn that a mere three percent of Americans own 95 percent of our privately held surface land. Even more concentrated is the ownership of oil, natural gas, coal, iron, and other raw materials. One man, Ted Turner, owns two million acres, nearly twice the size of the state of Rhode Island. In many cities a few families own most of the prime downtown sites. Land monopoly is alive and well in America.

Home ownership provides a kind of cover to this reality. Homeowners with their typical small lots are landowners of a sort, although mortgage lenders hold over half of the equity in their properties. Home ownership is a good thing, contributing to family and community stability. Those who cite the degree of homeownership as a gauge of economic well-being, however, are mistaken. West Virginia with its high poverty rates boasts a 76 percent rate of homeownership, highest in the nation. This masks the fact that, like a banana republic, the bulk of that state's rich natural resources are owned by absentee corporations.

Many parts of Latin America, Asia, and Africa suffer from exaggerated forms of land monopoly. The masses are beholden to small ruling classes typified by extensive landholdings and tremendous wealth. The United Nations reports that a mere 500 individuals earn more than 416 million of the world's poorest people. America is moving away from its egalitarian past and witnessing a rapid move toward great economic disparities. This wealth gap is not simply a measure of disparate annual earnings, nor of the miles-apart assets of rich and poor families. It is a reflection of the increasingly concentrated ownership of the land on which the economy stands, or totters. It is a flashing warning signal.

Clash of Ideals and Practice

America's land policies violate the noble ideals we profess. We recite our fundamental precepts but unconsciously permit them to mean something else:

All are endowed with inalienable rights to life, liberty, and the pursuit of happiness. But the lands necessary to activate these rights are increasingly concentrated in the hands of the few, diminishing the rights of the rest of society.

Equality for all, special privileges for none. Except that land monopolists drive a wedge between the overprivileged few and the growing ranks of the underprivileged.

People are entitled to the fruits of their labor – what they sow, others may not reap. But landed interests take unfairly large bites out of the earnings of workers and producers.

Thou shalt not steal is a Commandment we endorse. But we permit owners of prime urban sites that are required for commerce and the owners of natural resources that are essential to industry to siphon off land values that belong to the community as a whole. We imprison those who commit minor thefts but we protect by law, and tend to honor, those who take away the earth rights of their fellow citizens.

Custom, in short, has numbed people into accepting the landowners' privileged status.

Owning and Selling Air and Land

Suppose a man claimed to own the air and refused to let others breathe it until they paid him. His sanity would be questioned for claiming what he had no role in creating and for saying, in effect, "Pay me or die." Land, like air, is a provision of nature that nobody can live without. Yet our legal system is out of sync with this fundamental fact.

An owner might insist, "I got my land fair and square and I have a clear title to it." A search may trace that title back to a grant from

Congress, a king of England, or the pope who, sight unseen, assigned New World domains to the Spanish and Portuguese. None of these grantors, of course, obtained a prior grant from the Creator of the land.

This is not to question the need – nor the genuine virtue – of giving people exclusive rights to the *use* of land for their homes, farms, or business sites. Rather, it suggests the need for a mechanism that respects both the private use of land and the equal right of all people to nature's bounty. As described in the next chapter, such a mechanism exists but is too rarely put into practice.

The Injustice in a Nutshell

To challenge the notion that all people have equal rights to land is to argue against the hallowed concept that all people are born with equal rights. It is to claim that the life-nourishing qualities of land and the ability of land to bestow economic prosperity may properly be concentrated in the hands of a relative few instead of serving all members of society.

Not only individuals and families suffer from the misappropriation of land rights. Governments, on behalf of all citizens, also have legitimate claims to land that are not being recognized. Failing to collect their fair share of the land values created by nature and by their own activities, governments short change themselves. Then, to make up for their lack of funding, they over-tax the privately created earnings that rightfully should be left with workers and producers.

Compounding this injustice are the individuals, businesses, and so-called financial wizards whose mad pursuit of rising land values produces the bubbles and blows them up to the bursting point, utterly disrupting the economy.

European settlers brought their unfair land system to our shores. For several centuries Americans were largely inoculated against the harm of this system because of a most fortunate circumstance. The pioneers and settlers had *easy access to great expanses of free or cheap land*. Difficult as it often was to eke out a living on this land, its availability opened the way to almost unlimited job opportunities and kept our enterprise system free.

Once this happy circumstance was no longer the case, a greatly increased population had a harder time finding home sites and work sites. Unwholesome land tenure practices multiplied. Quintessential features of the American society – class mobility, a can-do attitude, and competitive free markets – were put into jeopardy.

Far ahead of his time, Philadelphia native Henry George, journalist and self-taught political economist, spotlighted this threat to our social fabric in his 1879 masterwork, *Progress and Poverty*. George's contention that there were serious cracks in our socio-economic foundation was seriously disputed in his day, and long after. Today few would deny that the country is beset with serious troubles. Yet the general public and our leaders reveal great confusion about the nature of those troubles and what to do about them.

Faulty Diagnoses

Not only did the most celebrated public affairs spokespersons fail to foresee the latest economic nosedive; after it arrived, most of them failed to ascribe satisfactory explanations to either the boom or the bust. Few cited land problems. Instead, they blamed soaring housing prices, unsafe mortgage lending, greed, mass psychology, and exotic investment devices. These were all sore points, but to a large extent each represented *referred pain*, as when a patient feels a severe ache in a thigh that is perfectly healthy but is painful because of an inflamed nerve in the spine.

The so-called housing price bubble was referred pain from a *land* price bubble. Few realized that home prices remained fairly stable throughout the cycle. It was the cost of the sites under those homes that were figuratively going through the roof.

The unsound economic behavior stemming from mass psychology and the greed of financial "geniuses" was transferred pain from vision defects that prevented people from seeing that there had to be an end to the steep climb in real estate portfolios, which is to say *land* portfolios.

The pain from the failure of the investment market was blamed by one camp on under-regulation and by another camp on over-regulation. Neither camp addressed the referred pain from *perverse land policies* that distorted markets and sent them into paroxysms. Neither those who defend the *free market* nor those who want to restrict it seem to recognize the extent to which the market is far from free, for reasons that are discussed later.

In economics no less than in medicine, focusing only on the referred pain is perilous. Operating on a healthy but painful knee, for example, makes the matter worse if the cause is elsewhere. Giving crutches, drugs, feeding tubes and other stimuli to various facets of the economy without treating the land policies at the source of the troubles will not keep the destructive effects at bay.

Such patchwork measures will set the stage for another wild ride on the roller-coaster unless there is a systemic treatment of the land system – the topic of the next chapter.

The Great Spirit Speaks[1]

I have given you lands to hunt in,
I have given you streams to fish in,
I have given you bear and bison,
I have given you roe and reindeer,
I have given you brant and beaver,
Filled the marshes full of wild-fowl,
Filled the rivers full of fishes;
Why then are you not contented?
Why then will you hunt each other?
I am weary of your quarrels,
Weary of your wars and bloodshed,
Weary of your prayers for vengeance,
Of your wranglings and dissensions;
All your strength is in your union,
All your danger is in discord;
Therefore be at peace henceforward,
And as brothers live together.

NOTE

1. From Henry Wadsworth Longfellow, *The Song of Hiawatha*, Grosset & Dunlap, 1923.

2

'Secret' Remedy
that Works

THE LOWER THE TAX ON LAND, *the higher its price. The higher the tax, the lower its price.*

These counter-intuitive but dynamic facts provide clues for fixing what is wrong with our economy. Armed with this insight, a select number of cities began reducing taxes on the value of housing and other buildings, while shifting more of the tax burden onto the value of the land, thus giving an incentive for making improvements. By retooling the property tax in this way, they started to achieve the revitalization that the rest of urban America has been seeking.

Remarkable Results from a Tax Change

By applying this "secret" remedy, many Pennsylvania jurisdictions achieved the following uniformly consistent results:

- Most homeowners won tax breaks.
- Businesses sprouted up on idle business district sites.
- Boarded-up shops and housing units were fixed and put back into use.
- In-city development created new jobs.
- Sprawl was retarded or suppressed.

- Neighborhoods were stabilized as their housing was kept affordable.
- Local treasuries in the red were soon in the black.

As detailed in Chapter 28, the achievements of these cities, all in the state of Pennsylvania, reveal that a corrective to our land tenure system is waiting in the wings, ready to be adopted. To repeat, the remedy calls in essence for *shifting property taxes off homes and other structures and onto land values.* The reform is known as the *two-rate tax.* This differentiates it from the conventional property tax that imposes a single tax rate on the *total* land-plus-building value. (For further explanations, see Appendix E.)

Cities that pioneered this reform of the property tax began modestly. At first, they imposed a tax rate on land that was only two or three times higher than their tax rate on improvements. As residents saw their property taxes stop increasing and even go down and as officials saw the old resistance to property taxes diminish, these cities further reduced tax rates on buildings and raised them higher on the value of land.

By 2009 Harrisburg's tax rate on land was six times higher than on buildings. In Clairton the land rate was 13 times higher than the improvement rate. All but eliminating the tax on improvements, Washington (Pennsylvania) and DuBois taxed their land values at a rate 29 times higher than buildings. Most homeowners in these cities enjoy lower taxes while holders of idle or underused sites in prime locations see substantial increases. The two-rate reform is reducing tax bills for 58 percent of property owners in Altoona, for 73 percent of those in Titusville, and for 91 percent of those in Allentown.

In short, modernizing the property tax to accord with a sound understanding of land economics has been tested. It works. It is evolutionary, not revolutionary, phased in at whatever pace is deemed appropriate for local circumstances.

Of course, this remedy is not really secret. It only appears so because it has been receiving the silent treatment for so long, with little serious attention in professional public finance circles or in the popular media.

Beyond the Property Tax

The *land tax* part of the formula looks like the indispensable missing piece of the puzzle for anti-tax politicians and their followers, who offer no alternative to funding the public sector. Their anti-tax stance leads them to take an anti-government stance. This tends to make them at a loss when it comes to satisfying the majority of citizens who still want excellent schools for their children, police protection, national security, highways, and the rest.

Anti-tax ringleaders claim the free market will make everything turn out fine if government will just get out of the private sector's hair. They forget that the almost totally unregulated economy of the 1800s did not prevent frequent runs on the banks, business failures, major unemployment, and nationwide panics. They forget that the free-wheeling private economy under blatantly pro-business administrations of the 1920s were the preface to the disastrous Great Depression. They forget that the deregulation supported by Federal Reserve Chairman Alan Greenspan was, as he himself belatedly admitted, a big mistake. What they forget makes them part of the problem.

This is not to blame the market. America's market system has never been fully free. Many corporate monopolies are based on control of vital natural resources, stifling competition. Powerful minority interests disrupt the workings of the market by raiding and manipulating land values, depriving enterprisers, workers and government alike of their rightful earnings. Government compounds the problem by failing to tax back the land values it helps to generate. Thus, to fund its basic function, government instead dips deeply into the wages of individuals and profits of businesses, further impeding the market. Capital is diverted from production to the pursuit of publicly created land values, which starts each cycle of artificial land bubbles. Is it any wonder, in the face of such irrational and chaotic distortions of the productive system, that markets do not seem to work?

A leading guru of the anti-tax camp, the late Milton Friedman, was pressed to say how governments should be financed. He grudgingly admitted: *"We need taxes. So the question is, which are the least bad taxes? In my opinion the least bad tax is the property tax on the unimproved value of land, the Henry George argument of many, many years ago."* [1] However, I find no evidence that Friedman ever promoted this "least bad" tax.

The anti-tax camp often appears heartless because, when public treasuries are short-changed, programs to help the needy tend to be the first to be cut back. People in this camp need to be shown that the value of the land under their homes, businesses, factories and shops is largely a reflection of the public works and services that make these locations desirable. It is difficult to imagine a more equitable or logical source of public funding than these publicly created land values.

Most officials, economists, and citizens in the opposite camp – those calling for more public expenditures – stress compassion for the needy. Too few of them, however, do better than the anti-tax camp in distinguishing between private and common property. They seem unaware that the types of high taxes they support and the public programs they devise often exacerbate the joblessness, poverty, and other problems they are designed to alleviate.

Here is a reality-based but clearly oversimplified scenario of how that works. Corn farmers are in trouble. Aid to them increases feed prices for pig farmers. Then aid to pig farmers disadvantages those who raise cattle. So ranchers get aid that boosts food prices that hurt the poor, who are given food stamps and housing allowances. Welfare subsidies tend to translate into higher rents, which hurt lower-income people like teachers and police. Aid to them requires higher local taxes that put marginal firms and people out of work. To create jobs, subsidies are given to new businesses, which make it harder for older businesses to compete. Soon this evolves into a regimen of aid to almost everybody. Then big corporations, large agribusinesses, and wealthy homeowners – those whose campaign contributions make them super-represented in Congress, state legislatures and city halls – walk away with the most generous public welfare, while the truly needy get mere crumbs.

Both the pro-tax camp and the anti-tax camp thus condemn America to repeat the boom and bust cycles that hurt our society. To avoid the incongruousness of their present stance, both camps would be well advised to consider how the tax shift formula cited at the start of this section could serve their goals.

Transition

The suggested tax shift is a far cry from current policy. How might we get from here to there? One of the first orders of business to achieve this transition should be the launching of an intensive public education campaign on land ethics and land economics.

Property tax revision is essential before land taxation can become feasible. The destructive part of the property tax – that is, the payments based on the value of homes and other improvements – needs to be greatly reduced or eliminated. The constructive part – taxes based on the value of lands and resources – needs to be greatly magnified. Then the increased taxes on socially created land values need to be matched by greatly reduced taxes on labor and production.

Gradually recycling the land values generated by public facilities will increasingly meet the costs of building, repairing, and operating our public works. This will begin a process whereby infrastructure can become largely self-financing.

Land value gains, misnamed as *capital* gains in the federal tax code, should be taxed as heavily as possible and certainly should not be given favorable tax treatment.

Federal grants should be designed to encourage land value taxation by states and localities. For their part, cities and states can use land taxes to wean themselves off reliance on federal funding and to regain more control of their own destinies.

This brief sketch is fleshed out in Part VII. It provides a suggested blueprint for getting from here to there.

Taking Your Property Away?

In case talk of land rights sounds frightening, threatening, or confusing to those who are unfamiliar with the concept, let's hasten to clarify the reforms that are being discussed and analyzed.

1. **This is *not* a proposal to confiscate individual or company property.** So long as property holders pay their annual land value taxes, their right to the exclusive use of their sites will continue to be secure, the same as it is now for those who pay their property taxes.

2. **Nationalization of land is *not* advocated.** Converting private lands into public ownership would be counterproductive in most cases.

3. **The profit motive and enterprise system will *not* be weakened.** On the contrary, they will be strengthened by lifting tax burdens off producers. The land tax will provide a more hospitable climate for those in the private sector who are engaged in the creation of goods and services, safeguarding them from killing land costs.

4. **Tax burdens for the majority of taxpayers will *not* be increased.** Most people's taxes will be reduced. Their higher land taxes will be more than offset by lower taxes on their homes, business structures, and other assets and earnings.

5. **This is *not* "land reform" in the sense in which the term was used in many poor countries.** Those places decreed government-enforced redistribution of lands held by the rich to landless people. The poor who acquired land often went into debt and forfeited their lands back to big landholders. Using police powers to redistribute land runs counter to everything this book favors.

What justice requires is an equitable sharing of the land's *value*, not the land itself, and this, as will be shown, makes a world of difference.

NOTE

1. As reported in the *San Jose Mercury News*, November 5, 2006.

3

What Is This Thing Called Land?

DEFINING LAND would seem too obvious to dwell upon were it not for the fact that land as an economic factor has been nearly obliterated by the fashionable theories of the past century. Since exploding land values have played a role in nearly every American boom, and since a collapse of these values touched off nearly every bust, it is timely and imperative to define land carefully.

What is land? How does it differ from private property? What gives it value?

Common Property

In everyday conversation, *land* conjures up images of farmland. It is that, too. In a modern economy, urban lands and natural resource lands play more prominent roles. A few square feet in a city's central business district are usually worth many times the value of acres of pasture on the outskirts of that city. Land *quantity* should not be confused with land *value*. Small areas of land may be extremely valuable, large areas may be almost worthless.

Land encompasses the entire *natural world*. It includes rural and urban sites plus the soils, quarries and wild game on the ground; the oil, gas, minerals, and ores under the ground; and the space and electro-magnetic spectrum used to transmit communications above ground. To underscore this critical point, land in an economic sense includes *everything provided by nature*.

Because nature's gifts are in no sense made by any one or any combination of individuals or governmental units, they are properly regarded as *common property*.

Private Property

Private property, in contrast, encompasses things *people* create. Food, clothing, shelter, and the myriad array of man-made products are private property belonging not to society in general but to those who produce them, buy them, or are given them. Put another way, private property results from applying human labor, skills, and ingenuity to land. Examples clarify the distinction between common property and private property:

- Oil in the ground is common property. Oil that is drilled, refined, and transported is converted by people's labor into private property.
- Fruit growing wild is common property. Collecting it makes it the private property of those who pick it to eat or to sell. Fruit in orchards on the other hand is the private property of those who plant, cultivate, and harvest it.

Blurring these distinctions has monumental consequences, as illustrated by two clashing political systems. Communism fell into disarray by erroneously classifying almost everything, including what individuals grew and produced, as common property belonging to the state. Capitalism *as currently practiced* is in difficulty because of the opposite error, a tendency to classify almost everything, including gifts of nature, as private property. "As currently practiced" is emphasized because the economists who literally defined free market capitalism – Quesnay, Adam Smith, John Stuart Mill, and David Ricardo, among others – recognized private and common property as distinct from each other and therefore requiring different treatment.

An old spiritual warns, "Everybody talkin' 'bout heaven ain't goin' there." Similarly, everybody talking about private property as the foundation of our enterprise system ain't goin' there either. Americans who claim common property as their own private property mistakenly suppose they are benefiting from free enterprise capitalism when, in fact, they are reaping the rewards of a special privilege.

Owners who held their homes for several decades congratulated themselves on their financial sagacity as their property assets escalated a thousand percent or more. Their gains resulted not from their brilliance but mostly from community growth and a false sense of scarcity caused by intense land speculation. Lucky owners sold before the bubble burst. Unlucky ones bought just before it burst and watched their assets plummet to less than the value of their mortgages.

USUFRUCT

Thomas Jefferson said, *"Land is held in usufruct by the living."* "Usufruct" means in trust. Jefferson understood that land differs from private property.

An owner of private property acquires nearly absolute rights to its disposition by virtue of having brought it into being (or by acquiring it fairly from others who created it). Ethically, the owner may use it, use it up, give it away, or destroy it, provided only that in so doing his or her actions do not interfere with the equal property rights of others. Because land is held *in usufruct* as the heritage of future generations, those holding it have a moral imperative to preserve and enhance it.

Location, Location, Location

These are the "three" things, according to the familiar cliché, that explain land prices with values that range from almost worthless to gold-plated. To better comprehend why some locations are worth more than others, however, one must pay attention to the chief factors that determine value: nature, people, and government.

Nature endows locations with a huge variety of unevenly distributed features. These include soil fertility, salubrious climate, and water for drinking, irrigation, and industrial use, to name a few. People willingly pay more for places where natural elements make life more productive, profitable, or enjoyable.

People passively generate land values simply by virtue of their presence and their numbers. In sparsely settled Podunk, land sells for a song. The cost is a bit higher in small college towns like Berea, Kentucky, but much higher in metropolitan centers like St. Louis or Denver. Site values there, in turn, are dwarfed by the value of sites in crowded Chicago and Manhattan. The greater the concentration of people, the higher the land values.

People also generate land values in an active way through the totality of their enterprise. The quality of their residential and commercial buildings, the vigor of their market activity, and their creation of amenities all affect the productivity and attractiveness, and thus the value, of lands in their neighborhoods.

Government services and facilities leave a trail of land values in their path. People readily pay more for neighborhoods protected by good policing, enhanced by trees and clean streets, served by quality schools, and endowed with quality transportation. Parks, playgrounds, water systems, bridges, convention centers – in fact, almost all government provisions – tend to raise the value of the sites they serve. We say "almost all" because some useful public facilities – like a refuse dump or an airport's noisy flight path – negatively impact the price of adjacent lands.

True and False Values: The Speculation Factor

Nature, people and government account for *legitimate* differences in land prices. If these factors told the whole story, the message of this book would not be pertinent to civilization's quest for a more just society nor to halting the cycle of recurring economic crises.

Unfortunately, genuine land price differentials are overwhelmed by *fictitious* values arising from *land speculation*. This damaging practice pushes land costs much higher and throws a monkey wrench into land markets, distorts land use patterns, and disrupts the normal working of the economy. How so?

The dynamics may be illustrated by speculators John and Jane, doing business as J&J Holders. They buy half a dozen prime central city lots, hoping to profit from their anticipated future jump in value. Mary and Bill, who run M&B Builders, envision a development on one of those lots. However, J&J, eyeing a killing a dozen years hence, sets a price so far above current prices that this effectively takes that lot off the market. This shrinks the supply of available sites, enabling owners of comparable sites to raise their prices.

Eager as M&B was to locate in the city center, it settles for a cheaper second-rate site where the firm will produce less, hire fewer employees, and gain lower profits. Other developers are also discouraged from locating in the central business district. Land owners in second-rate locations then see a surge in demand for their lots and they up their prices too.

Soon development is pushed to third-rate and fourth-rate city sites, then out to suburbs and beyond into farmland – not for lack of close-in sites, but because speculation priced those sites out of reach.

Since the supply of land is fixed, *artificial* shortages of available sites translate into *actual* land price increases, based on no change in real value. Yet the easy profits made by land speculators induce still more speculation and the cycle mounts.

Why emphasize *land* speculation? In a society with open competition, speculation in *products* – unlike harmful runaway speculation in land – tends to be beneficial. The crucial difference is that the supply of most goods is not fixed, so the supply may contract or expand. When speculators withhold a product from the market and thus raise its price, others see a chance to profit by making this product more cheaply. As they get into the act, the resulting competition tends to increase the availability of this product at reduced prices. Consumers win.

Land speculation offers no such self-regulating feature because competitors cannot create new land or import it from elsewhere.

The stresses that land speculation imposes on metropolitan areas are not minor. It drains population and commercial activity from central cities. It drives leading stores and other commercial activity to outlying malls. By forcing businesses into less productive sites and by distancing workers from work places, it contributes to joblessness and poverty. It is one of the primary reasons for the sprawl that forces duplication of infrastructure, wasting time, money, and energy. It puts new home buyers and new enterprises at the mercy of land monopolists.

AN ANALOGY

A football stadium may be likened to a metropolitan area. The best locations – luxury boxes and seats close to the 50-yard line – are comparable to the central business district. People pay top dollar for these seats. People who want to pay less get seats in the bleachers. All spectators see the game at prices that vary in fairly direct proportion to the desirability of their view of the action. This is true unless scalpers buy up quantities of desirable seats. When the ticket office says "No seats available", scalpers descend on fans, taking advantage of the artificial shortage they themselves created, demanding many times the original price.

Scalping at the stadium is unfair. It cheats and upsets customers. Sports club owners try to prevent it. But this scalping is peanuts compared to the large-scale scalping of home sites and business locations. Land speculation scalping disrupts local economies, ignites recessions and robs millions of a fair seat in the game of life.

Urbanologists who analyze critical metropolitan issues without reference to land speculation are reminiscent of astronomers who charted the skies when they still believed the planets revolved around Earth. Those astronomers drew planets going through contortions, interrupting their orbits with a series of curlicues, called epicycles, while circling the Earth. Those charts seem unbelievably ridiculous today. Although their sense of relationships was not totally wrong, they missed the true pattern by failing to understand that the sun was the center of the planetary system.

Similarly, those who attribute the decline of cities to the automobile and highways, to federal and local policies favoring new development over old, or to corrupt politics are not entirely wrong.

These elements clearly play a role and require attention. Yet the true orbits of these other forces are misconstrued when the central role of land policy is left out of the picture.

The Trick of Sharing Common Property

Ancient peoples tended to be enlightened about the need to share common property. This natural understanding was almost put out of mind as civilizations became more complex – and for understandable reasons. People had not figured out fair ways to turn the concept into reality. How could all the people in a community exercise their equal rights to common property, including *your land*, without interfering with your private property, such as your home, your shop, or your garden on that land?

This dilemma led people to make protection of private property their top priority and to sweep thoughts of common property rights under the rug. When the landless poor lived in hovels in the shadow of luxury – the large estates and palaces of Indian rajahs, the chateaus of France, or the castles of British lords – they were cowed into believing inequality was the natural order.

The most articulate response to this dilemma was provided by Henry George. He was not the first, by any means. When the United States was in its infancy, the British economist David Ricardo threw light on the subject by formulating the law of rent. Long before that, the prophets of biblical times were outspoken in blaming the misery of the poor on the excessive privileges of the landholding rich. However, by zeroing in on the friction between common and private property rights, George illuminated a key issue that eluded many other social thinkers. Once grasped, it is eloquent in its simplicity:

> **Rights to common property** are obtained by sharing the *value* of the land, not by physically carving up or redistributing the physical land itself. That value, collected by government through a land tax, may be used to provide services and facilities to all citizens and firms, with any surplus distributed as cash payments to everyone in the jurisdiction.

> **Rights to private property** are secured by leaving the returns from it in the hands of those who create it.

This is almost the reverse of present policy. We unjustly allow privileged individuals to cream off common property values while governments get the bulk of their revenues by tapping into portions of people's private earnings and private property.

A just society requires treating both common and private property equitably. A land value tax regimen meets this criterion. No mere tax gimmick, it is a prescription for social justice. For those unfamiliar with the concept, following are some points about how it works and why it will be beneficial to adopt it as soon and as extensively as possible.

Under a land tax ...

- The value of any unit of land reflects its advantages relative to all other units at a particular time. This assumes no false speculative values, a fair assumption because a substantial land value tax will return most land value gains to the public. This wipes out the speculators' *raison d'être*.
- Owners of highly desirable locations repay the public for their special privilege – represented by the annual rental value of their land. These payments, transformed by government into public goods enjoyed by all, indemnify those who lack access to choice locations. Thus everybody shares in the benefits of land and resources.
- Owners of undesirable sites pay little or nothing in taxes but enjoy the public goods financed by the taxes paid by holders of valuable sites.
- A further equalizing feature is that excess revenues, beyond those required for public needs, may be distributed as citizen dividends to every man, woman and child.
- Paying annual taxes based on the worth of their lands gives owners exclusive use rights and security in their holdings. As with today's real estate taxes, if you pay, you stay.
- A rigorous land value tax changes economic incentives. It makes land *using* more profitable and mere land *holding* much less profitable. Land holding that suppresses job growth gives way to land use, which fosters job creation.

These points harmonize with and reinforce the American ideal of *equal opportunity for all*. In the tradition of our nation's earliest leaders who wrestled with how to make democracy work, Henry George wrote, "We cannot safely leave politics to the politicians or political economy to college professors. The people themselves must think, because they alone can act."

PART II

EMBARRASSMENT OPENS A DOOR

As the following chapter illustrates, Ralph Waldo Emerson was so right when he wrote, "We know that the secret of the world is profound, but who or what shall be our interpreter, we know not. A mountain ramble, a new style of face, a new person, may put the key in our hand."

4

Newsroom, *Columbus Citizen,* 1951

"CITY DESK, RYBECK."

"My name is Kathy Shoaf. I'm calling to request an announcement of an economics course sponsored by the Henry George School. I'll be teaching it at the YMCA next month."

"You said Henry George? Could I ask, is your school accused of being subversive?"

"Absolutely not. We want to strengthen America." She bristled and her voice was shaky. I was embarrassed that my abrupt query had upset her.

Ms. Shoaf had no way of knowing that my intention was to take the community's pulse, so to speak, because my head was spinning from a bitter controversy I had been reporting on for weeks.

Ohio State University, my beat, was caught up in a troubling battle. OSU's president and trustees were engaging in what turned out to be a prelude to McCarthyism. They spied on instructors and took lecture quotes out of context. They spread fear with rumors that the campus was infiltrated by Reds or Pinkos – names that, during the Cold War era, implied friends of the Soviets and foes of America. To block subversive influences, they imposed a "gag rule", requiring professors to get permission before they could invite off-campus experts to speak to their students. When the president refused to let A.J. Muste, a well-known pacifist, address a sociology class, incensed faculty members went public, charging an assault on academic freedom. As this elevated into a national story, I found myself competing with reporters from the *New York Times, Chicago Tribune* and the wire services to track all the charges and counter charges.

Keeping up with more seasoned reporters was not my only concern. Writing even-handedly about the controversy as faculty, alumni, and people around the nation took sides on the gag rule was a challenge because my editor, Don Weaver, wholeheartedly supported the university administration. To his credit, he never asked me to alter or tone down my reports, many of which included arguments 180 degrees from those in the editorials he was writing.

Getting back to Ms. Shoaf, she had no way of knowing, either, that she ignited my memory of an economics professor who devoted perhaps a few minutes to Henry George and dismissed him as a wrong-headed idealist of the Progressive era. So hearing his name triggered an image of someone far from the main stream.

My query was a clumsy attempt to see how much the red scare on campus had permeated the Columbus community at large. Once I realized Ms. Shoaf mistook my question for an accusation, I assured her that was not my intent. Truly curious, I said I would put a notice about her class in the paper and then try to attend it myself. Which I did, but the experience did not go smoothly.

In college I had studied economics theory with Valdemar Carlson, a Keynesian, labor economics with Lewis Corey, a fiercely anti-Marxist ex-Communist, and the interaction of politics and economics with John Sparks, a constitutional specialist. With that background I felt rather qualified, after skimming the class readings, to dispute Ms. Shoaf's presentations. The biggest hurdle was my inability to accept her insistence on the pivotal role of land in the economy, an idea that was alien to anything stressed by my professors or that I had encountered in my readings.

Yet I admired Kathy's respect for opposing views and even more her volunteer work with the area's multiple sclerosis sufferers (she advocated for them and arranged wonderful parties for people with MS and their families). So I agreed when she asked me to drive her and two associates to Montreal for an international Henry George conference. They offered to pay for the gas, no small inducement in a day when journalists were near the poverty class. It struck me as an opportunity to pursue my ornithological interests. I hoped to spot Hudsonian Curlews and other birds known to thrive on the mud banks of the St. Lawrence while Kathy and her friends talked economics.

"The best laid plans..." I looked in on the conference, got intrigued and never did see my birds. Did I suddenly see the light while exposed to lectures by Henry George's followers? Not at all. What fascinated me in the talks and discussions was a refreshing contrast to the stultifying conformity that prevailed in central Ohio during that Cold War era. The conference attendees seriously questioned the underpinnings of society, political ideologies, and conventional thinking about peace and war. What philosophy or perspectives, I wondered, united this disparate group of Georgists whose professions ranged from stock brokers to farmers, from teachers to preachers and attorneys?

Curiosity about that assemblage, what made them tick, led me to devote the next couple years to studying their theories and analyses of social maladies. My chief mentors were Robert Clancy, head of the New York Henry George School, who oversaw branches around the country, Verlin Gordon of the Ohio branch, and Robert Benton of the Detroit branch, who commuted to teach in Ohio.

Many others shared their knowledge with me as I wrestled with their unfamiliar concepts. Joseph Stockman, director of the Philadelphia Henry George School, who was steeped in Chinese philosophy, never let discussions get too serious. Rupert Mason, a California bond specialist, told how he helped revolutionize the financing of irrigation districts in his state. Perry Prentice, a Time-Life publisher, brought public attention to urban land issues in *House & Home* magazine. Woodrow Williams, a rough-cut self-taught Ohio farmer, was a wise friend and teacher. Professors Harry Gunnison Brown and Mason Gaffney were among the few profes-sional economists seriously focusing on land taxation in the 1950s. Vi Peterson, originally from England, executive secretary of the Robert Schalkenbach Foundation, used her diplomatic skills to unite disparate Georgist groups in America and around the world in a period when most of the tides were inhospitable to their reform ideas, which is putting it mildly.

Before I could agree with the Georgist overview, I was forced to unlearn or put in different context much that I had gleaned from college courses and journalistic forays into economic matters. Yet, the more I delved, the more convinced I became that George's ethical orientation and reliance on scientific methodology could resolve problems that otherwise seemed insoluble. And the more I appreciated my good fortune in answering Kathy Shoaf's phone call.

The next section traces influences along my intellectual journey, helping to explain why the Georgist message eventually began to resonate with me and shape my life's work. My hope is that telling these stories will enable others to more easily grasp the conclusions I reached.

PART III

A JOURNEY
OF ECONOMIC
DISCOVERY

DEEPLY EMBEDDED IDEOLOGIES of our times initially led me to reject the centrality of land policy and the inequitable treatment of land wealth elucidated by Henry George and others. This power of accepted standards and customs to sustain themselves with little questioning lets us understand how our predecessors could mentally block out past injustices like slavery or denial of women's rights. It explains how socially aware and intelligent people have difficulty in recognizing ethical fault lines in our current economic landscape. The following chapters describe the constellation of people and events that shaped my economic perspectives and gave me a sense of urgency about getting America back on track.

5

The Earth,
Our Home

WHAT NATURE PROVIDES – this bountiful earth – is the ticket to survival and well-being for every person and creature in the world. How much longer we can abuse and poison the air, water and soil of our earthly home and workplace is no idle academic question. More and more people have come to agree with the noted ecologist and ethicist Aldo Leopold (1886-1948), who wrote: "When we see land as a community to which we belong, we may begin to use it with love and respect. There is no other way for land to survive the impact of mechanized man." Or for mankind itself to survive, it may be added.

Starting in the early 1930s, A.B. Brooks, a charismatic naturalist-philosopher and pioneer conservationist, led bird walks every Sunday morning in my home town, Wheeling, West Virginia. My parents, Ry and Buddy, were faithful A.B. followers – literally, along the beautiful trails of Oglebay Park.

A.B. organized nature leadership camps every summer, two weeks at Oglebay and two more in wilder parts of West Virginia. From the ages of 11 and 12, my older brother Art and I were allowed to participate in these adult programs. The faculties included the renowned bird artist George M. Sutton; herpetologist Graham Netting, the future head of Pittsburgh's Carnegie Museum of Natural History; Maurice Brooks, chair of West Virginia University's Forestry Department, a botanist and specialist on Appalachian culture; plus geologists, astronomers, and entomologists.

In a mountain camp alongside Lake Terra Alta, the evening vesper songs of the Veery resounded in the woods like a symphony of flutes and left a permanent imprint. Identifying ferns, trees, wild-flowers, birds, reptiles and so forth was not the point. The natural-ists' quest was how plants, animals, soils, insects and rock strata related to each other and to humans. Ecology was their "in" word, unfamiliar to few outside their circle at that time. Not content to dwell on what was known, these nature leaders seemed always in hot pursuit of unraveling nature's mysteries – how migratory birds navigated, or how leaves converted sunlight into energy, for instance.

Gentle, dignified A.B. and his circle were radicals. They were rebelling against scientists who had "gone indoors", so to speak, confined to their labs and losing touch with the natural world. While winning public acclaim for their marvelous new inventions and products, at times they were unintentionally putting at risk the intricate and fragile support systems developed over eons to sustain life, including human life.

As to America's "march of progress", A.B. recalled seeing huge flocks of Passenger Pigeons darkening the sky during his boyhood. Beech tree branches on which they roosted broke from the load. Hunters killed them by the thousands, yes, thousands, to put on dinner plates and to feed their hogs. By 1914 the Passenger Pigeon was extinct, ahead of other species being wiped off the face of the earth.

Older campers told how lumber companies felled every accessible tree in the Allegheny Mountains, clear-cutting almost all of West Virginia's magnificent old-life forest. Without trees and under-growth to hold back the water, floods became more prevalent, rich fertile soils eroded away, and rural people living off foods grown on nutrient-deprived soils suffered poorer health.

During his Sunday bird walks, A.B. helped hikers single out the "instruments" in nature's symphony – Indigo Bunting, Wood Thrush, Tufted Titmouse, Kentucky Warbler, Carolina Wren, and other songsters. He had an actor's knack of making his favorite poems come alive. It became evident from the philosophers he quoted that our forebears' intimate association with the beauty and wonder of nature etched important elements into the American character.

One Sunday A.B. discussed nature's restorative powers, noting how the scouring of streams rushing over gravel and sand, along with the life forms within them, formed a water purification system. But he said this remarkable cleansing capacity was being defeated by mines and industries that overloaded rivers and tributaries with more impurities than they could tolerate.

"I have a confession," spoke up a local steel executive. "The State Legislature passed a law against acid pollution, so we stopped draining acid directly into the Ohio River. We dug large pits to collect the poisonous liquids. When these pits fill up, we call state inspectors to watch us dump the acid all at once, and pay our fine. We just considered the fine a cost of doing business." He shook his head saying, "There must be a better way"

Association with A.B. enabled me to become curator of Oglebay's nature museum and a nature guide for day campers during my teenage summers, and embarked me on a lifetime of awe and delight.

Perhaps A.B.'s most enduring gift to those touched by him was an understanding that we humans are land creatures, part of an interdependent web of living things. Respect for this web, difficult as it may be for a society that no longer has its feet on the soil, is essential for the health and sanity of the human race. As Chief Seattle said about this web, "What we do to the web, we do to ourselves."

For those who bemoan the prospects for major social reform, A.B.'s pioneering work offers an optimistic lesson. From small beginnings, the Oglebay nature camps and the Brooks Bird Club became prototypes for the Audubon Society, the Sierra Club, and others. Gradually environmental awareness spread nationwide, blossoming into a political movement with considerable clout.

6

Land of Opportunity

FOR A NATION overwhelmingly populated by immigrants and their descendants, we pay precious little attention to what made America a land of opportunity, not just for the few but for almost everyone. My grandparents' story is not unique. In the telling of stories like theirs, the emphasis understandably is on how hard the immigrants worked and sacrificed to enable their families to prosper. Rarely mentioned, however, is the role that real estate or land played in their struggles to get ahead.

My grandfather Heyman Rybeck left the pogrom-ridden Polish-Russian border region in his late teens, crossed the Atlantic, arrived alone and penniless at Ellis Island a decade after our Civil War, joined a synagogue, picked up an approximation of English while working in leather shops, saved enough to buy a candy store in Manhattan, and married Hungarian immigrant Fanny Greenwald. They raised three daughters and two sons and lived above the shop, sharing a bathroom with other families on their floor. When the children were old enough to see over the counter, they pitched in to help their parents serve customers long hours every day.

Heyman contracted tuberculosis, recuperated on a New Jersey farm, and later retired to suburban Mount Vernon in Westchester County. The family grandly referred to that house on Homestead Avenue as "the homestead". Heyman got disability payments from a Jewish burial society, a kind of insurance in that era, but he and Fanny survived mainly from the large portions of their paychecks that four of his working offspring regularly sent home.

The eldest, Nancy, became a fashion writer on the *New York Daily Mirror*. I was about to say, "with only a high school education". Would that only a high school education prepared children so well today. Nancy spoke with a lovely theatrical style, not a trace of her parents' heavy accents. She was well read, loved the arts, and had a keen interest in public affairs.

Samuel, my father, was next in line. Known as Ry, he graduated from the free City College of New York and served in World War I. An apprenticeship in Gimbels led to his becoming advertising manager for a small store in New Jersey. He and Nancy helped their younger brother enter the advertising world and Maury soon became a rising star at big name stores. Flo was a dress shop saleswoman. Ruth, the youngest, was still at home.

Tedious work and cramped living conditions were the lot of many immigrants, but they recalled that their families had endured similar hardships or worse in the Old World. There they felt doomed to remain in poverty. Here their poverty was merely a first stop, a springboard. Examples of friends and neighbors working their way up the economic ladder showed that keeping one's nose to the grindstone, so to speak, really paid off. People who only partially realized the promise of upward mobility put their hopes in their children's prospects.

The idea that everyone had a chance to earn the good life so permeated the atmosphere they could almost taste it.

How did real estate figure in this story? Land was cheap enough – even in America's largest city! – for folks like Heyman to gain a foothold in business. Acquiring space for a song, he became his own boss. As he and Fanny proudly watched their family flourish, no payments to landlords and no income taxes whittled away their earnings. The harder they worked, the more they could earn and save. Their one tax on real estate – the property tax that current political demagogues love to impugn – funded the superior school system and other municipal services that contributed to New York City's attraction.

Granddad rhapsodized about how American freedom blessed his family. His patriotism overflowed when he and Grandma joined us on a trip to Washington. I saw tears streaming down Granddad's face as we climbed the Lincoln Memorial steps and he confronted that pensive face on the statue of the Great Emancipator.

Years later, during visits to my grandparents, when my father's old friends gathered, they would frequently voice a lament. If only their parents had held on to the Manhattan lots they once owned, they sighed, their families would now be rolling in wealth. Why, they asked, had they not been like the Astors, never selling land and growing "filthy rich" from the gigantic rise in New York real estate prices? It never occurred to me in my childhood days to question why these folks felt they should have become millionaires simply by holding on to a piece of land. Nor did I wonder whether the people who had become extraordinarily rich due to no productive effort on their part did so at the expense of others who actually created that wealth. At any rate, my parents' friends, by laboring in their various professions, had carved out reasonably comfortable lives. Was that not a good thing and sufficient?

It should be underscored that America was a land of opportunity, not merely because people worked hard. People work hard, often extremely hard, in almost every country in the world. What made our nation so special was that it provided easy access to affordable places to work and because it did not erode away the rewards of that work via high rents to landlords or a multitude of injurious taxes.

7

The Call To Make
a Better World

DO RELIGIOUS LEADERS have a role to play in ending joblessness, poverty and recessions? American clergy and lay leaders were slow to take a stand against civil rights abuses. Many even defended and promoted such abuses. Yet, once the churches and synagogues belatedly got on board the cause of the blacks, there was no stopping or turning back the movement for their equal treatment. When religious leaders and organizations take strong stands against injustice and make them a moral issue, they prove to be a powerful force for good. Where do they stand on today's social disorders and abuse of land rights?

Unlike Granddad, who wore his talis or prayer shawl every morning, swaying as he chanted Hebrew portions of the Scriptures or Talmud, my parents were Reform Jews. Dad at times served as president of our congregation. Mother, Rosalind Greenbaum Rybeck, known as Buddy, headed our religious school. We attended Friday evening services and celebrated Jewish festivals. We also enjoyed the festive spirit and non-religious aspects of Christmas. Brother Art believed in Santa Claus longer than many of our little Christian friends because he had "seen him" – a Santa impersonator who caught him sneaking a look for presents one Christmas Eve. On occasion, Dad led the lighting of Wheeling's community Christmas tree.

Our rabbi in the 1930s, George Lieberman, taught that the vital core of our religious heritage was ethical monotheism. One God, therefore one humanity. Typical of teenagers, we questioned the miracle stories. The rabbi said we could choose to take them literally or poetically. But he was not permissive about the Bible's moral lessons. Society's problems were caused by people, not God, and therefore it was up to humans to resolve them. Our ethics, he taught, should imbue us with a determination to correct injurious behavior and to be peacemakers in our families and the larger community.

The rabbi's teachings, fortifying the similar views of my parents, made me feel a common bond with people of other religions, and with those who claimed to be agnostics or atheists, for that matter, as they tried to find their paths in the world and reached out to make a better world.

Our social climate reflects an undercurrent of unfairness that leads to excesses of belligerence and unsustainable disparities between the very wealthy and the very poor. People who find inspiration from religion should feel challenged to correct public policies that are out of kilter – including the inequitable sharing of nature's gifts – and champion more ethical approaches. Don Marquis (1894-1937), journalist, poet and social satirist, wrote shortly before the Great Depression: "The gods do not make men better. And when men have made themselves better, the Almost Perfect State will be here – just like that."

8

That's Business

WE ROMANTICIZE SMALL BUSINESSES although, to a greater degree than we like to admit, we have become a land dominated by mega-firms. The official federal definition of "small" is a stretch. Companies with up to 499 employees or that gross up to $6,999,999 a year are classed as small businesses. Yet a number of genuine mom and pop businesses do still exist. The rules by which small businesses operate – not the legal framework but the ethical codes determining how they treat employees and customers – set the tone for relationships among families, communities and society. The microcosm of my parents' small business illustrates the point and underscores why land policies that could give small enterprises greater leverage would be so desirable.

Dad was an instant success when, at age 50, he opened an interior design business. A couple would come to Rybeck Studios to buy a Venetian blind and end up redecorating their whole house. Dad and Mother enjoyed serving affluent clients, but their biggest joy was working with young lower-income couples and helping them, often over the course of years, to have homes that fit their incomes and surpassed their dreams.

This "instant success" was based on years of solid experience. After apprenticeship in New York and New Jersey, Dad became advertising-sales manager and vice president of Stifel's, Wheeling's second largest department store. Adept at human relations, community relations, and customer service, he made Stifel's profitable, even during the Depression. To enable store clerks to be home with their families on Christmas Eve, he led a successful campaign to close all Wheeling stores early on that day.

When Stifel's president, pretty much a figurehead, died, the chain that owned the store overlooked Dad, despite his excellent work, and brought in an outsider to fill the position. That was business, said the managers in the New York headquarters.

Dad then turned a friend's faltering dress shop into a flourishing venture. Seeing this success, the local newspaper, which held the bankrupt Palace Furniture Store in a receivership, hired Dad to revive it. Short-handed, Dad asked Mother to join in his rescue efforts. As quietly sedate as Dad was exuberant, she protested that she had never sold anything, but Dad persuaded her to act as hostess. Soon her good taste plus a knack of judging what styles suited different customers made her the star salesperson. Mother also wrote a weekly newspaper column, "Inside the Palace". In lieu of conventional ads, she wrote about decorating trends, interesting customers, or goings-on in the store, like a "Palace romance" between two employees.

The Palace gave other local furniture stores a run for their money. The largest competitor conspired to have out-of-town financiers buy out and close down the Palace. Mother discovered that a man they had known for years had engineered this. She asked him how he could do such an underhanded thing. "That's business," he replied casually. Mother detested that excuse and often recalled it as the type of ethical lapse that gives business a bad name.

Dad, used to landing on his feet after setbacks, typified American optimism. At this point he risked opening Rybeck Studios, his own business. He and Mother were as good to their staff as to their customers. They trained them so well that Gene and Irene, the couple that had fallen in love at the Palace, were able to take over and run the store after Dad died.

Many 8-to-5 workers do not realize how their work lives differ from that of their small business bosses. Mother and Dad worked late evenings and weekends to keep their enterprise viable. They befriended manufacturers at furniture markets. They negotiated long and hard with sales representatives so they could compete price-wise and not lose customers to big-city stores in Pittsburgh, sixty miles away.

My parents' mix of civic involvement and business brought them economic security, a wide circle of friends, and a rich life. They boosted Oglebay Park and its nature program. Mother started the park's day camp. They actively supported the symphony, international folk festivals, hospital committees, and family service programs. Dad loved acting. Once, when the amateur theatrical group's usual theater underwent repair, the play in which Dad starred was moved to a school auditorium. The sign on the highway in front of St. Michael's Catholic school announced the performance in large bold letters: "THE BISHOP MISBEHAVES – 7 PM ALL NEXT WEEK."

Words cannot convey the depth of my parents' fondness for Wheeling, for West Virginia's beautiful hills, and for their country and the opportunities it provided.

Wheeling, however, was undergoing a transformation, and not for the better. Through World War II, the city was the bustling tri-state hub for rural and industrial towns up and down the Ohio valley, east into Pennsylvania and west into Ohio. Then factories shut down one after the other. Leading stores left the city, fading away or popping up in outlying malls. Population dwindled. Fine buildings were torn down for parking lots. The formerly active B&O and Pennsylvania Railroad lines closed down and their rails rusted. Crime, poverty, and unemployment grew.

Given these trends, Dad located Rybeck Studios not downtown but "out the Pike", on the other side of a hill from the business district. My brother Arthur moved his dental practice to a residential neighborhood when patients no longer felt safe in his previously fashionable downtown site.

It was no consolation that similar problems were afflicting cities throughout the Rust Belt and beyond. Officials in Washington, state legislatures, and city councils seemingly had no clue about the causes of this downward spiral or what to do about it. Many West Virginians, after years of being exploited by resource monopolists, became resigned to being in an economic backwater.

Working hard and smart, my parents managed to keep their business viable, but it greatly pained them to watch as friends and associates fell victim to the worsening local economy. Art, imbued with his parents' sensitivity and community spirit, responded to bad times by devoting his weekends to offering free dentistry to poverty-stricken folks in the area.

"Doing well is the result of doing good," wrote Ralph Waldo Emerson. "That's what capitalism is all about." Monopolists who restrict competition are not "doing good". Shops are boarded up, cities decline and unemployment increases. Meanwhile, people who do well financially tend to hunger for more and more income, perhaps because they are unconsciously fearful of joining the underclass. If prosperous people were not islands in a sea of poverty, is it not conceivable that they would be satisfied with less copious incomes and inclined to pursue non-monetary enrichment for themselves, their fellow workers and their communities?

9

War or Peace?

IF, AS MANY BELIEVE, war is inevitable because of an inherent fault of human nature, the potential for mutual nuclear destruction hangs over us. My strong feeling, however, is that survival of the species is a more primal drive and that this drive can prevail when our collective intelligence is enlisted in the pursuit of a peaceful world. No small part of this challenge is correcting arrangements that deny decent living conditions for so many of the world's people.

Days before I became a soldier in 1942, Sara, a Quaker friend, asked how I would feel if I had to kill someone. It struck me as an odd question. Japan's attack on Pearl Harbor had filled us with pro-war frenzy (the word is not too strong). Belligerent dictators in Germany, Italy and Japan and a demonic Nazi plan to obliterate the Jewish people fed our conviction that we had to fight to save our country, our European and Asian allies, and civilization itself.

No war hero, luck was on my side. I moved from an anti-aircraft outfit at Fort Bliss, Texas, to engineering training at Oklahoma A&M, to the infantry in mid-Texas, to the combat engineers in a Mississippi swamp, to Morse code training at Fort Belvoir, Virginia. Our battalion went overseas late in the war. Crossing the English Channel at night, a depth charge alarm sent all hands on deck – except for me, sound asleep on the top of a stack of six bunks. I awoke as the all-clear signal brought troops back to quarters.

We were stationed behind the lines at Epernay, France, instructing other troops in our specialty, assembling pontoon bridges. After Germany's defeat, we were set to sail from Marseilles to the Pacific when atomic bombs led to Japan's surrender. We veterans, saved from further combat by those bombs, have a more benign view of the bombs than do later critics. Our ship made a U-turn back to the U.S.A.

Interestingly, I had chosen *War and Peace* from the ship's mini-library on the way to France. Tolstoy did not soft-pedal war's brutality and carnage, and he portrayed the bewilderment and lack of control by generals in both Napoleon's and Russia's armies. I must have persuaded myself that his account applied to *that* old war, not ours. It was frightening to learn later how close Britain came to being overrun, how totalitarianism nearly triumphed. We were spared by German mistakes, by Britain's staying power, by the spunk of ordinary GIs, by America's industrial might, by the Russian front, and by superior Allied strategies.

In Epernay a Jewish couple, Gaby and Gaston Hannaux, befriended me during the last months of the war. Gaby had come out of hiding. Gaston had escaped from a labor camp, where his translating abilities had made him useful to the Germans. They lived above their fur shop, from which their equipment and furs had been stolen. Gaby's cousin Odette told how Nazis, angered by local resistance, randomly picked a dozen men, lined them against a wall and shot them. They were bullet-ridden beyond recognition, but Odette found her husband's wedding band on one of the bodies.

Such heartbreaking stories, plus tales of German atrocities in World War I, plus more horrors recalled from wars in the 1800s, made me pessimistic that French-German enmity could ever be healed. How could the old men, women, and children I watched scavenging our garbage dump recover from the ravages of war? Greater cause for dismay about man's inhumanity to man struck me when I visited a buddy in a hospital in Rheims and caught a glimpse of concentration camp survivors – emaciated living skeletons. Their memory still haunts me.

Nothing I saw, heard about, or experienced prepared me for the surprising aftermath. Europe's foes united. The Marshall Plan, a mix of American idealism and practicality, had a healing effect, uplifting Western Europe's economies and deflecting ancient animosities. Within a generation France and West Germany cooperated in coal and iron production, helped form a common tariff union, eased border restrictions, joined a European parliament, and adopted a common currency.

The atom bomb's immense power had stunned mankind. Some thought it would change everything, signaling the end of war forever. Wrong. The bomb reinforced whatever people believed before the ominous mushroom clouds arose. Nationalists became more so. Internationalists and pacifists became more so. Militarists became more so. In the guise of defense, the United States and the Soviet Union vied to acquire the best and largest arsenal of nuclear weapons, converting the post-war years into the Cold War. Nuclear proliferation remains a most troubling issue of our times, notwithstanding the heroically patient efforts of scientists and statesmen to edge world leaders and our own hawkish militarists toward a sane disarmament posture.

My three years in the army fortunately were on the outskirts of the war. That was close enough to see the horror and mayhem it wrought and the obliteration of centuries of cultural treasures. That was personal enough to have lost friends killed at Pearl Harbor and in the European and Pacific theaters, and to see a brilliant classmate become psychologically damaged from hardships he endured in the Battle of the Bulge.

War also has its tragicomic aspects. My father and my wife's father fought on opposite sides in World War I. The war medals Erika's father won in the Austrian army did not keep him and his wife from being persecuted by his own countrymen and murdered by Hitler's henchmen. My Dad's only apparent residue from that war was to occasionally put my brother and me to sleep by singing taps, "Day is done, gone the sun, from the lakes, from the hills, from the sky, all is well, safely rest, God is nigh."

On a recent anniversary of the dropping of the atomic bombs, Erika and I dined with a native of Nagasaki who was miraculously unharmed while her family members died of radiation burns. After a career in treating bomb victims, she married an American and came to the States. We smiled – to keep from weeping – at the oddity of how a shattering event affected us so differently but did not stop us, decades later, from rejoicing in our common humanity.

Could the massive killings, destruction of cities, lost treasures, and other tragedies of the worldwide conflagration have been avoided if, instead of waiting until after the war, we had committed before the war a genuine concentration of good will, energetic diplomatic efforts, and capital investments? Obviously, that was no longer an option once Germany, Italy, and Japan were intent on aggression. Long before, however – in the immediate aftermath of World War I – could not something akin to the Marshall Plan have been initiated? Can civilization move to a stage in which nations learn to wage peace with the same fervor that they wage war?

Gandhi's passive resistance campaign to free India from British rule intrigued me as a step in that direction. Should not America take the lead in mounting strategies of diplomacy and economic cooperation to defuse international friction? Martin Luther King, Jr, a student of Ghandi and Thoreau, wrote: "To meet hate with retaliatory hate would do nothing but intensify the existence of evil in the universe. Hate begets hate; violence begets violence, toughness begets a greater toughness."

The need to reverse civilization's race toward mutual destruction was uppermost in my mind as I returned to my studies. Forging America as a pro-peace anti-war force struck me as a challenge of monumental importance. It was some years before I became aware of the extent to which struggles for control of land and resources pitted nation against nation. Achieving an equitable distribution of land rights to ease poverty, unemployment and homelessness – and to erase the bitterness and enmity these induce – will help foster the peaceful world that now seems almost beyond our reach.

10

A Glimpse
of Utopia

CERTAIN TIMES AND PLACES open up vistas where life is liberating, happier and more stimulating. They give us a forecast of what society might be. Such a time and place for me was Antioch College in Yellow Springs, Ohio, after World War II.

Antioch was a blissful antidote to army life. The honor system was refreshingly civilized. Student community managers ran campus government so democracy was no mere ivory tower theory. Faculty-student work parties fostered community spirit. Without inter-collegiate competition or a star system, all students enjoyed sports. The mix of backgrounds – whites, blacks, Europeans, Africans, Asians, radicals and conservatives – helped us respect and celebrate our differences. The students, mostly war veterans, were eager to make up for lost time and their hunger for learning led them to discuss the day's lectures long into the night.

Antioch's unique features reflected the philosophy of engineer-educator Arthur E. Morgan, president emeritus during my years on campus. After a 1913 flood took hundreds of lives and caused massive damage along the Great Miami, Little Miami, and Mad Rivers of Ohio, Dayton leaders called on Morgan to prevent future disasters. His five dams were first called "Morgan's follies" because they formed no lakes. Apertures at the bottom of the dams were large enough for normal river flow. Only when the rivers were swollen with heavy rains or snow melt were excess flows forced to back up. Strange as "dry lakes" looked, downstream cities and industries have been flood-free ever since. Morgan designed an equally unique financing plan, using a species of local land value tax with no federal funding. (This plan is described in "Paying for Infrastructure – Miami Conservancy of Ohio" in Chapter 28.)

Morgan's reputation as the country's preeminent river valley engineer led Roosevelt to name him as the first head of the Tennessee Valley Authority. TVA was multi-purpose, designed for power generation, navigation, and recreation as well as flood control. Morgan integrated all these features to regenerate a poverty-stricken sector of Appalachia. TVA became the New Deal's stellar success.

Morgan shifted his focus to education after one of his dam sites near Dayton required relocating and combining two towns, Fairfield and Osborn, into a new city called Fairborn. During this socially disrupting task, he found his staff well-trained technically but poorly equipped to deal with human relations. To cultivate political and social skills, Morgan conceived a novel educational approach and searched for a college to try it out. Antioch, founded in 1853 by Horace Mann, was on the market. Morgan's innovation was the co-op or work-study program. Vocational training was a secondary goal, the primary goal being to help students understand and get involved in community life while on their jobs.

If students were to be trusted to act responsibly on jobs around the country, they needed to be able to supervise themselves off campus and on campus as well. Unlike most colleges in that era, Antioch did not act as a nanny. Hence the honor system on campus. Students bought supplies in the untended bookstore, leaving what they owed in a kitty. They set their own hours. They took open exams back in their dormitories.

Founder Horace Mann had challenged Antioch students: "Be ashamed to die until you have won a victory for mankind." Arthur Morgan challenged students to fashion society in accord with their highest goals, inspiring them to replicate the school's mores and values. In my mind, Morgan's eminence as social reformer and ethicist equaled his genius as an engineer.

I conspired with Kenneth Hunt, biology professor and director of Glen Helen, Antioch's thousand-acre nature preserve. We organized Sunday morning bird walks, opened the Glen to school camping, and held nature leadership weekends for townspeople, students, and faculty.

Eating in the Kitchen

Coretta Scott was one of my closest college friends. She was an aspiring singer before she married Martin Luther King, Jr. Hearing her tell about the indignities her family suffered while she was growing up in Alabama was heartbreaking. Black churches around Ohio invited her to sing and I went along as accompanist. Mixed-race couples were seldom seen in those times. We were never physically harmed as we traveled by bus – but if looks could kill! We were relieved to reach the churches, where the audiences invariably received me with the same warmth as Coretta.

Lest people forget the racial climate in America in the 1940s, an incident is worth recalling. I invited Coretta and two other students to an Oglebay folk dance festival in my home town, led by folk leader Jane Farwell (herself an Antioch grad and another of my role models). We arrived in Wheeling in time for dinner with my parents at the 12th Street Grill. The manager nodded toward Coretta.

"She'll have to eat in the kitchen."

"That's completely unacceptable," Dad protested.

"If it were up to me, she could join you," he replied, seeming to forget that he was the manager as he shifted the blame. "It would upset the customers."

Years later Coretta cited this incident in a book, saying she ate in the kitchen while the rest of us ate in the dining room. I can only guess that an editor persuaded her that this misstatement would better dramatize the evils of segregation. The truth strikes me as a better story. We phoned the festival and asked if any dinner was left. Plenty, they said, but they had just cleared the tables from the dance hall. So we drove to Oglebay Park where *all of us ate in the kitchen!* The folk dancers reached out to Coretta and fell in love with her, not erasing but taking the edge off the demeaning treatment she had suffered downtown.

Coincidence

One of Antioch's all-time favorite professors, philosopher George R. Geiger, had a sparkling humor – the honey that made his medicine go down. The "medicines" were his probing questions about the meaning of life and taking responsibility. Later, when I was a reporter in Columbus and took that Henry George class, I learned to my surprise that Geiger's father, Oscar H. Geiger, had founded the Henry George School and that Prof. Geiger himself had written *The Philosophy of Henry George*, a gem of a book highly praised by John Dewey and written fifteen years before I was in Geiger's class.

I went back to campus to ask Geiger why he never mentioned this in his courses. Henry George, he told me, was so derided in the 1930s that philosophy societies blackballed Geiger for promoting George's ideas. He said he did not abandon his views of social justice, but he very consciously took care *not* to cite Henry George.

I also learned that his interest in philosophy, as well as in Shakespeare and the theater (he was an accomplished amateur actor), was spurred by his father. During his high school years, Oscar Geiger organized a literary club for his son and some of his bright buddies. Several in this circle achieved fame, including Harry Golden, editor of the *Carolina Israelite*, a quirky but widely read small newspaper, and author of *Only in America*. I was able to locate eight members of that group and help set up a reunion. After that, Geiger lost his reticence about Henry George. When our paths crossed, he would press me, "Are we making progress with the land tax?"

Transradio Press

I got fired from my first co-op job, at Transradio Press in New York. TP had grown rapidly during the war years with its one brilliant idea. Other press services were adhering to an old journalism formula, telling the whole story in the first paragraph. Radio announcers turned purple trying to read who, what, where, when, why, and how in one breath. TP came to their rescue, writing the news in short punchy sentences.

That smart idea was too easily copied. When I arrived as a TP copy boy, I was unaware that the United Press and Associated Press had installed their own broadcast divisions, adopting TP's style to win back radio clients. I thought it was my brilliant writing that led the editor, after my very first week, to invite me to become night editor. That meant rewriting each day's late news to make it sound fresh for morning broadcasts. I asked if I could start a week later while I crammed on the national and international news that I had lost touch with during my war years and while on campus. He agreed. Yet two days later, perhaps frustrated by his rapidly sinking ship, he fired me. That did not hurt as much as his parting shot: "You're not cut out for journalism." TP went out of business a few months later.

I quickly found an office typing job until it was time to return to campus. Getting fired early in my career turned out to be liberating. My world, I soon realized, had not collapsed. Thus, in later jobs, I never worried that I had to shave my convictions for the sake of my livelihood.

A Very Different New York City

It now seems like a fantasy. I often went to an eatery near TP called the Exchange Club. On the way out, a cashier by the door asked us what we had eaten and rang up the charges on his cash register. In midtown Manhattan this busy restaurant operated on the honor system. Ah, 1947!

Antioch demonstrated the potency of vision. The college I knew was very much the reflection of the vision of Arthur Morgan. Without vision, civilizations decline; with it, they can progress.

11

Dreams of
a Castle

TO KNOW WHERE we're going, especially if we're trying to improve social conditions, it's essential to know where we're coming from. So I am indebted to a small-town editor who shared his passion for American history. Other interesting developments, there in the heart of West Virginia coal country, arose from unexpectedly spotting a castle.

My first real newspaper job in Fairmont could not have been better. Some evenings *Fairmont Times* Editor E.C. "Ned" Smith, in a melancholy mood after a Scotch or two and missing the son he had lost in the war, would invite me into his office for a chat.

He reminisced with pride about his maneuvers at the 1932 Democratic convention to help nominate Franklin D. Roosevelt. Then he would ask, "Are you paying attention to America's First Team?" He was not talking sports. He was referring to the genius of Washington, Jefferson, Adams, Madison, Franklin, and other Founding Fathers. A serious history buff, Smith observed that revolutionaries who rise up against tyranny are a dime a dozen. After toppling old regimes, most become tyrants themselves. The remarkable thing about our First Team, he said, was that they gave power to the people, not to themselves, and that they devised a way to guarantee both minority rights and majority rule.

My work in Fairmont as an Antioch co-op began during the 1948 presidential campaign. I often heard Smith order banner headlines featuring Dewey's attacks on Truman's handling of the presidency.

As it was widely predicted that Dewey, the Republican candidate, would win, I had the temerity to ask why he gave these orders. "Boy," he said, "we want Democrats to get mad enough to come out and vote." They did, to many people's surprise, but not to Smith's.

Routine

Journalism is often painted as exciting and glamorous. My tasks included writing obits, getting weather forecasts, calling the hospital for new births, listing club speakers, carrying typed articles to Linotype operators, and helping proof the galleys. One day, to counteract boredom, I combined weather data and newborns in a jingle. After that, my silly rhymes appeared daily in a corner of page one.

A short-handed news staff was my good fortune. City Editor Sutton Sharp asked me to cover a tax evasion case in federal court against "Big Bill" Lias, the gambling king of Wheeling, my home town. The first day's legal wrangling between the prosecutor and defense lawyer utterly confused me. I threw myself on the mercy of the court, confessing my puzzlement to Judge Harry Evans Watkins. He clarified significant points and invited me to come to his chambers whenever I had questions. I had stumbled onto a valuable technique that I gladly share with beginning journalists: when writing about unfamiliar topics, seek out experts who can help you give readers a fair interpretation of issues and events.

The Greatest Newspaper

"You're with the *Fairmont Times*, Walter? You work for the greatest paper in the country." Was Van Bittner, whose speech I was covering, pulling my leg? Detecting my disbelief, he asked me to join him for a beer so he could explain.

Bittner was a mineworker organizer back when unions were forbidden. To get around that prohibition, Bittner became a minister. He preached to get workers' ears about unsafe mines, cheating by company stores, and scales that undercounted the coal that determined each miner's wages. A real war erupted with armed camps firing at each other. In a front page column, Editor Smith proposed a temporary government takeover to get mines back into operation. Bittner penned his opposing view and got a courier to cross hostile line to deliver his letter.

"The next day I couldn't believe it when I saw my rebuttal on the front page," Bittner said. To his astonishment, Smith's columns and Bittner's answers alternated every day for several weeks. "No other newspaper was this fair to labor," he said, supporting his "greatest paper" comment to me.

Failure's Surprising Fruit

One day I crossed the bridge from downtown Fairmont to a residential area across the Monongahela River and was stunned to see a romantic reddish castle. At close range it seemed less romantic, with its broken windows and tangled shrubbery. I learned that a man named Hutchinson, who made a coal fortune during World War I, took his wife to Scotland where she fell in love with Inverness Castle. What does a coal baron do? He builds her a replica, moat and all. Oldsters recalled how the castle lights were all ablaze when West Virginia and Washington bigwigs, brought to Fairmont in chartered trains, were lavishly entertained there.

After Hutchinson died, his attorney, Judge Shaw, bought the castle from his widow. Shaw made no secret to me that he disapproved of the Hutchinsons, contrasting their sumptuous lifestyle with his own frugality. I asked a relative of Shaw's if he might let the castle become a community center. She thought the retired judge was purposely "letting the castle rot to show people the wages of sin". Yet Shaw let me inspect it with a contractor, and his cost estimate for restoration was not excessive – it was an amount local groups might feel justified in raising in exchange for making the castle their home.

We failed to save the castle. Many clubs and organizations were enthusiastic about the project, but Judge Shaw would not co-operate. A decade or so later, when I took my wife to Fairmont, all we could see of that fine replica of Inverness Castle was a pile of rubble.

Out of this failure, however, came an unexpected result, the founding of a symphony. While pondering how to stir interest in the castle, I ran into a close family friend, Dave Daniels, in front of a jewelry store. He was an accomplished Polish violinist who had been the Wheeling Symphony's concertmaster. Under a New Deal program, Daniels was chosen to form and conduct an orchestra in Parkersburg. Federal funds stopped abruptly after Pearl Harbor and his orchestra folded. A relative in Fairmont offered Daniels a job as salesman in his jewelry store.

When I asked Davey if he still played violin, he shook his head. "They just like hillbilly music here," he said. Not true. I had already met others who enjoyed classical music. One was Thelma Loudin, a school music supervisor, who told me that, as a little girl, she had played violin in the castle's great hall. She remembered being awed by displays of medieval armor there.

At any rate, I wrote a short news item inviting anyone eager to play chamber music to meet at the YWCA. Instead of the half dozen we anticipated, thirty showed up. We realized we had the makings of a symphony. Davey said he had loads of symphony scores. So we launched a search for missing instrumentalists.

Because Fairmont's Dunbar High had an excellent music program, l called on the principal to see if he could help us locate the musicians we needed. The response of that well-educated black man may sound incomprehensible to people born after the 1940s. "A symphony would do wonders to elevate the civic climate here," he told me. "Don't jeopardize getting it started by involving Negroes," he advised.

Seeing my disappointment, he explained: "Fairmont is funny. When I'm walking along the sidewalk, one white person will smile at me but the next one moves so menacingly toward me that I have to jump out of the way. We're always off balance."

The principal was trying to spare Fairmont's blacks from the rejections and hurts that tended to be their lot. However, our need for musicians took precedence over racial considerations. Several black musicians were willing to show up for the first rehearsal. Everyone was so delighted to be making music that no sign of prejudice broke the harmony.

As the group tuned up, a trumpet player who also headed the local musicians union warned that he and others were really rusty. "Not to worry," Davey said. "I'm not Stokowski, and we'll start with easy Strauss waltzes to break the ice." The musicians, plus the wives and husbands who had come with them, were almost in tears as the music swelled. Soon they gave their first concert and Davey became Fairmont's beloved conductor till the end of his long life.

The symphony was a splendid dividend from my failed efforts to save a castle. It inspired others who were interested in acting to ask me to help them start a little theater, which also took root. Such stories need to be repeated and remembered to counter the defeatist attitudes of would-be reformers who, though seeing the need for change, too often belittle their power to make a difference.

12

A Far Cry
from Home

A YEAR IN LATIN AMERICA became a kind of college course in land policies. There one sees land problems in exaggerated form, clarifying how land tenure and taxation policies sharply divide society into the wealthy few and the impoverished multitude.

While many college friends went on to grad school, I was eager to get on with a writing career. That, plus the willingness of my former *Fairmont Times* editor and three Ohio Valley newspapers to take weekly columns about South America, let me enjoy a year as a foreign correspondent.

A tramp steamer took me from Brooklyn to Barranquilla, Colombia, where it unloaded a cargo of dynamite. We went through the Panama Canal to the Pacific Coast port of Buenaventura, Colombia. The small fees from my newspapers, thanks to the dollar's amazingly favorable exchange rate in that era, financed my adventures in Colombia, Ecuador and the Galapagos Islands.

The title of my columns, "A Far Cry from Home", reflected the cultural distances as well as the distance in miles from Appalachia to Latin America. Yet my experiences in those places illuminated for me much about my homeland.

The Price of Order in Colombia

In Medellin, I asked a local editor why his country seemed to be witnessing an authoritarian takeover. He arranged a session with

59

executives of two textile factories and managing engineers from a hydroelectric project to respond to my query. They had all studied at U.S. universities. They exemplified the energetic enterprise that made Medellin people known as the *Yanquis* of Colombia. They took pride in Colombia's long period without revolutions and in their peaceful freeing of slaves. I wondered why they supported their new leader, who had a dictatorial bent.

"Laureano Gomez will make workers disciplined, as in your United States," a factory executive said. The others nodded in agreement. Worried by the awakening of a long subjugated lower class, these men defended use of police powers to duplicate what they had perceived as the "order" in my country. It saddened me that they admired an outward aspect of U.S. industrial relations. They seemed to have little inkling of the long struggle by tradesmen, and by mine and factory workers, to overcome the overwhelming power of owners and management, and to gain government protection of their basic rights – rights that Gomez was starting to repress.

This session often came to mind as Colombia spiraled downward, as rebels and militia locked in battles that killed many of their country's finest jurists, journalists and statesmen, and as Medellin became known, not for its industrial prowess, but for its vicious drug cartel.

Ecuador's Half Truth

"We're a rich land and a poor people." Ecuadorians from all walks of life could have been describing my West Virginia as they voiced what I came to think of as their national mantra. This mantra however was a half truth.

Rich land, true. Ecuador's treasures included fertile valleys, vast tropical forests, and an ideal climate for bananas, coffee, cocoa and the *jipijapa* palms from which Ecuadorians laboriously made the straw hats known incorrectly as Panama hats.

Poor people, both true and false. Grinding poverty was the norm amidst Ecuador's rich resources, but the mantra omitted the controlling fact that the few who controlled the land – and thus the economy and the political machinery – were incredibly wealthy.

In my interview with Galo Plaza Lasso, Ecuador's handsome president, he said modernization was his recipe for easing poverty. Galo Plaza's family owned thousands of hectares of his country's best farmland. This was no surprise. Most accounts of Latin America refer to vast rural haciendas. What I was not prepared for was the extent of *urban* land monopoly. I was told, for example, that most of central Quito belonged to the Jijon family, whose lavish mansion I visited adjacent to the cathedral.

Most of my young Ecuadorian friends, in their twenties and thirties, called themselves communists. Why? A typical reply: "Ecuador has tried capitalism and it doesn't work." It did not look like capitalism, certainly not the U.S. version. The parents of these young radicals were eking out a living in downtown shops and paying over half of their earnings in rents to the Jijons. Like the peons getting meager wages on Galo Plaza's estates, the shopkeepers were operating under an almost feudal system. It seemed fairly obvious that rampant landlordism was making Ecuadorians susceptible to communist demagoguery. A thin veneer of capitalism was struggling to exist in the face of an oppressive system of land monopoly. My friends there seemed unable to see it that way.

Utterly Foreign

A few things completely unknown to me back in the States were commonplace in Barranquilla, Buenaventura, Cali, Medellin, Bogotá, Quito, Cuenca, Ambato, Guayaquil, and other cities I got to know in Colombia and Ecuador.

Omnipresent heavy iron grates. Merchants pulled them down over their store fronts at night.

Snarling watchdogs behind walls topped with jagged shards of glass. These protected homes in the "nice" neighborhoods. The grates and fierce dogs both bespoke a degree of fear and lawlessness I could not have imagined back home. Nor could I have imagined that the iron grates would become familiar equipment in our own cities all too soon.

Lottery sellers on the streets. All day long they cried out. The buyers, often shoeless, spent pesos needed to feed their kids. Poor laborers, apparently giving up on the world of work, put their faith in luck as a way to escape their miserable existence.

How could people condone raising public revenue by preying on such desperately poor citizens?

With no glimmer of shame, the officials I interviewed justified the practice by recounting worthy purposes such as welfare programs, hospitals, and schools that were funded by the lotteries. I would have objected strenuously if anyone had told me then that our own states would, within a generation, use this same logic to justify lotteries and other forms of publicly sponsored gambling. Or that our media and state governments would hype playing the odds to such an extent that it would whittle away at the work ethic in Americans' thinking and behavior.

My dismay was not a moral judgment against betting or disapproval of people who chose to amuse themselves with games of chance. Rather, I was struck that a nation was on mighty shaky ground if it had to finance its public goods and services by inducing those who were most in need of these goods and services to gamble away their pitiful earnings.

Many problems in Latin American societies that stem from land privileges are gradually taking hold in the United States. The growing gap between the haves and have-nots is one example. Rampant crime and insecurity in our cities is another. An increasing reliance on lotteries instead of equitable taxes to fund public services is yet another. It would not be prudent to think these trends can be reversed without addressing the underlying land issues.

13

Eden, Darwin
and Free Land

THE "REGULAR MONTHLY NAVY BOAT" I took to the Galapagos
Islands did not return for three months. Its delay gave me an
unexpectedly long and glorious stay on these islands a thousand
miles west of South America. They belong to Ecuador and lie
on the Equator. The cold Humboldt Current swirls up from
Antarctica, bathing the islands and modifying their temperature.

Ground doves were so tame they let me pick them up. To walk
in an extinct volcano crater amidst hundreds of Blue-Footed
Boobies was dreamy. Herds of sea iguanas came fearlessly within
inches. People shouting "thar' she blows" when whales surfaced and
exhaled a geyser came right out of Moby Dick. Imagine frolicking
in the breakers with sea lions and wandering among them on shore.
This peaceable kingdom inspires one to wonder if or when humans
would evolve to live as harmoniously with each other as do the
Galapagos creatures.

Understanding how living things evolve was the monumental
contribution of Charles Darwin. He was only 26 when his ship, the
Beagle, arrived at the Galapagos in 1835. Amazingly, he was not
overawed by the wonders there, as were other naturalists before and
after him, and as I certainly was (at the same age as Darwin when
he was there). Instead, he noticed and documented seemingly
picayune differences in the beaks and tails of a nondescript finch
and other minutiae as he moved from one island to another on this
archipelago.

Far from rushing into print with his suppositions about the cause of these differences, he spent the next twenty-four years gathering further evidence for what he had observed before publishing *The Origin of Species*. Incontrovertible evidence has piled up to confirm Darwin's core conclusions. Those who feel his scientific findings undermine religious beliefs one day may come to see that the way creatures and plants change is no less miraculous than the Bible's allegory of creation.

In my view, however, public debates over creation arguments divert attention from a more serious distortion of evolution theory, a theory posited by proponents of Social Darwinism. They twist one of evolution's mechanisms, survival of the fittest, to applaud the "fit" ruling class and people of great wealth, and to look without compassion on the supposedly "unfit" underclass. Justifying and comforting the exploiters of the world in this way does a terrible disservice to the evolution concept. Darwin's theories emphasized long-term adaptability and sustainability.

On the Galapagos, Blue-Footed Boobies dive for fish and hawks eat lizards, just as we too eat other creatures, although super-market packaging disguises this pretty well. The natural world is not all roses and honey, but neither is it all tooth and claw. Darwin recognized that the fittest species do not destroy their environment or food supplies but create conditions in which their young can survive.

A marvel of nature is that, although all plants and animals are part of a food chain (we are lunch for mosquitoes), the survival of each species also depends on symbiotic and cooperative relation-ships within their biological setting. By disregarding the role of mutual support systems as tests of fitness, Social Darwinians abuse Darwin's name and philosophy.

Galapagos human history is no less remarkable than its natural history. Getting to know some settlers and hearing the tales of how they came to live on the islands was fascinating. At Academy Bay on Indefatigable Island, I pitched my tent in the ruins of a cannery built by Scandinavians who turned to farming up the mountainside when their fishery venture failed. One of them, a Norwegian named Horneman, explained that the five populated islands in 1950 were each governed, like ships, by an Ecuadorian navy captain. The captains allotted land – free land – to residents for their homes, gardens, and animals. Mr Horneman admired this system that gave families as much land as they needed and could use, but no more.

Around the bay from where I camped, Carl Angermeyer and his brothers Gus and Fritz lived with their wives, all in little homes they themselves had built. Carl said they left Germany after Hitler came to power "because everyvone vas acting like sheep, and ve vanted to be men". With movie-star looks, they *were* men – admirable, kind, strong, and friendly.

Carl and his wife Marga took me on their boat to see many of the islands' natural wonders. They winked when I told them of my conversation with Horneman about land allotments. Old Horneman, they confided, had a reputation for "all talk and no work". I laughed, recalling that, while Horneman was leisurely taking the afternoon to share his philosophy, his industrious wife was pouring a cement floor in their home. The world needs thinkers as well as laborers, Carl conceded.

At any rate, the land policy Horneman described worked well enough when only dozens of families lived in rather primitive circumstances on the inhabited islands I visited. There were no paved roads, motorized vehicles, hotels, restaurants, or stores that exist there now. Barter was more common than monetary transactions. (In Quito I had met Margaret Wittmer, who had lived on the Galapagos since the early 1930s and who persuaded me to visit her family on Floreana Island. She gave me the good advice to take sacks of flour, sugar, and other staples to help pay my way with the islanders.)

The only motorized vehicle I saw there in 1950 was one truck used by the small contingent of Ecuadorian naval officers who guarded the abandoned airfield on Seymour Island. That facility was built by the United States during World War II, not to protect the Galapagos turtles or iguanas, but to exercise control over air space leading to the Panama Canal – our strategic lifeline to the Pacific.

Did the Galapagos system of free land hold up during the decades after my stay when new residents and merchants came to urbanize the settlements and cater to the thousands of international tourists streaming there? Economics students looking for a thesis topic ought to check it out.

Over eons, the Galapagos evolved, thanks to natural laws, to become a veritable wonder, an Eden. Can Americans discover the essential land-to-people relationships that can let us evolve into the just and equitable society of which our Founders dreamed?

ENSLAVED IN PARADISE

A captain unloads a shipload of people on an island with fresh water, abundant fish in the waters, decent soils and materials for building shelters. Did they land in paradise? After the ship leaves, they learn that a man in the big house up from the port claims ownership of the entire island. He says he will allow these people to use his wells, his home sites, his garden spots and so forth – with a little proviso. In exchange they will owe him whatever labor he prescribes. Dependent as they are on the use of his land, they have little choice but to accept the terms of their "host".

Theoretical? No, it is precisely what happened on the Galapagos island of Chatham in the late 1800s. Manuel Cobos won from Ecuador the right to collect an unusual lichen growing there, known as dyer's moss, which was much in demand for producing a reddish dye. To provide a workforce for him, Ecuador unloaded political prisoners at a nearby beach. In exchange for his water and primitive shelters, these unpaid workers gathered the lichen, tons of which were sent back to the mainland. They also cultivated sugar cane and food crops. Cobos treated his workers cruelly. I ate watermelon grown by descendants of those prisoners. They pointed out the Cobos plantation house and its balcony from which they said two slaves threw Señor Cobos to his death in 1904. An account of the trial of the murderers, in *El Telegrafo* in Guayaquil, told of a more brutal ending, claiming Cobos was hacked to pieces by razor sharp machetes in revenge for his having shot several workers dead.

Land injustice has a way of begetting more injustice.

PART IV

THROUGH A LAND LENS

EXPERIENCES DESCRIBED in the previous section eventually helped me to comprehend the problems of land monopoly and the virtues of land taxation as a just way to resolve our society's widening divide between the underprivileged and the overprivileged. As America's economic ills worsened despite immense public expenditures, my search for alternatives to prevailing policies intensified. Throughout my journalism and economics careers, it became increasingly evident to me that effective solutions required attention to almost forgotten land issues enunciated by Henry George and others.

Typical of most Americans, I had been unaware of our inequitable treatment of land rights. Once recognized, however, facets of our current land policies became a kind of lens that explained the nature of many social, economic, and political problems. Those who discover how these unjust land policies reach their tentacles into many realms of economic life have a catchphrase for this recognition: "Seeing the cat." The term harks back to a drawing of a tree in which a large cat is not immediately apparent among the branches but, once it is seen facing the trunk, it dominates the picture. The viewer cannot *not* see it.

Winston Churchill saw the cat. Early in his political career he wrote, "Land is a necessity of human existence and the original source of all wealth... Land monopoly is not the only monopoly, but it is by far the greatest of monopolies ... a perpetual monopoly and the mother of all other forms of monopoly... Every step in material progress is undertaken only after the land monopolist has skimmed the cream off for himself."[1]

Seeing the Cat

Many people read *Progress and Poverty* and immediately recognize its validity. Typical economics graduates, however, have been so immersed in contrary theories that its central ideas strike them as outlandish. No pun intended. When Dr Margaret Reuss, chair of the economics department of the University of the District of Columbia, saw the cat and came to realize how the misappropriation of land values was at the heart of the housing problems she was trying to ease, she exclaimed, "How did I ever get a PhD in economics without learning about Henry George?"

NOTE

1. *Liberalism and the Social Problem*, Hodder & Stoughton, London, 1909, pp.319-26.

14

Columbus –
Ode to a Bug

AFTER MY SOUTH AMERICAN ventures, an insect came to my aid. I was waiting for a job interview in the *Columbus Citizen* newsroom when a farmer brought in a jar containing an insect with an unusually long "tail". After the reporters all looked and shook their heads in puzzlement, I informed them it was an ichneumon fly. I said the so-called tail was an ovipositor used to drill through tree bark to deposit eggs that, when hatched, feed on and kill harmful beetle larvae. Orchard growers count the insect a fine asset, I told them.

Thank you, ichneumon fly, for winning me a job as reporter, feature writer and state editor.

The Slum Game

Blighted housing got national attention in the 1950s. My exposure to landlordism in Latin America led me to wonder who owned the slums in Ohio's capital city. I learned that among those renting wretched living quarters to the poorest of the poor were members of the school board and city council, bankers, and the pillars of churches and synagogues. They did so because it was profitable.

Due to the upside-down property tax, along with depreciation allowances and highly leveraged mortgage financing, owning slums was often more highly profitable than other investments. The more apartments or rooming houses deteriorated, the lower they were assessed and taxed. Rents from tenants covered the owners' tax bills.

Meanwhile, their holdings were growing more valuable, not for anything they performed but because of population growth and city improvements. The term "slumlord" has a bad connotation, yet most Columbus slum owners were regarded as upright citizens and astute real estate investors.

This raises questions for those who would like to rid their cities of slums. Is miserable rental housing the fault of the *owners* or of the *tax system*? This system makes slums a lucrative investment while it piles heavy financial burdens on owners who modernize and nicely maintain rental properties. The obvious next question is: whose job is it to change the system?

Walt Whitman, a poet of the Civil War era who was in close touch with the "common man" and the meaning of democracy, sensed the importance of access to land when he wrote: "The greatest country is not that which has the most monopolists, vast fortunes, with its extreme degrading poverty, but that in which there are the most homesteads, freeholds."

Accepted Rules

One Columbus man I'll call Mr G was playing an interesting land game. He studied the parade of people and businesses fleeing to the suburbs and methodically bought land all around the city. Whichever way expansion occurred, developers of tract homes, fast food outlets or malls first had to buy or rent from him. He positioned himself to become a kind of toll collector from the firms who were seeking places to locate their operations. As residents and businesses leapfrogged Mr G's holdings, his speculation also generated sprawl, blocking orderly development. For this he attracted no criticism but rather was recognized as a shrewd power player, respected for his considerable wealth.

At the time I was observing this, I learned that Sidney Evans, a land reformer I had known through Georgist organizations, had become a millionaire by following the same formula as Mr G. A native of Nebraska, Evans settled in San Diego and acquired land in the path of growth all around that city. How, I asked him, did he square this with his professed opposition to land speculation?

"We live in an unjust society," he replied. "If I didn't reap these rising land values created by the community, others would. I play by today's accepted rules, and then use my financial gains to persuade people to overthrow these unfair rules." True to his word, Evans indeed was a major benefactor of economic reform organizations that were devoted to promoting a more just land system.

In contrast, Mr G and scores of others who had become expert at working the "accepted rules" appeared more than satisfied with those rules and the enrichment garnered therefrom.

15
Dayton –
Ode to a Book

EDITOR WALTER LOCKE of the *Dayton Daily News* was walking me to lunch to discuss an opening for an editorial writer. He asked what I was reading and I told him I was intrigued by an old book, *Progress and Poverty*. On the crowded sidewalk, Locke, a lanky Lincolnesque man, threw his arms in the air and roared, "Oh no, not Henry George!"

After a bad moment, I realized he was toying with me. He confessed that Henry George had inspired him during his university days in Lincoln, Nebraska. Did he by any chance know my Nebraskan friend, Sid Evans? "Yes, we were in the same Single Tax club." (Some early supporters of George were known as Single Taxers.) I sensed that the job was in the bag when Locke added, "Nobody should be allowed to write about city problems until they've digested *Progress and Poverty*."

One No-No

I worked hard as a reporter to suppress my own opinions. Editorial writers, on the other hand, are in the opinion business and are expected to push their views boldly and persuasively. I asked Locke if there were limitations on what we could editorialize about. Locke said, "I'll introduce you to the Governor and you can ask him that."

The Governor was publisher James M. Cox, a former three-term progressive governor of Ohio. As Democratic candidate for president in 1920, with Franklin Roosevelt as his running mate, Cox campaigned on a pledge to support American membership in the League of Nations in order to heal the aftermath of World War I. Locke once wrote about this, saying Cox walked "open-eyed into defeat for the sake of peace". Defeating Cox was another Ohio publisher, Warren G. Harding, whose slogan was "back to normalcy". Besides his two Dayton newspapers, Cox by 1953 had acquired two in Springfield, Ohio, the *Journal* and *Constitution* in Atlanta, the *Miami News* and a number of television and radio stations.

"Just one thing," Governor Cox, then 83, replied to my query. "If my editors argued for public sponsorship of any form of gambling, I would be most unhappy." He said he had always opposed that because it infects government with unsavory elements. I recalled my dismay that Colombia and Ecuador used lotteries that bilked poor people while the elite won special privileges. I assured Cox that we were on the same page on that issue.

Mentor-in-Chief

Locke's daily column, "Trends of the Times", was admired for its wide-ranging tours of history, natural history, literature, and politics, and for its lyrical, almost biblical, style. He was among the first to nail the evils of McCarthyism. Calling innocent people "reds" gave cover to the small but dangerous clique of real communists, he wrote.

Born in a log cabin in 1875 near Nine Mile Ridge in a backwoods part of West Virginia's Pleasant County, Locke lived to witness the advent of the atomic age and space travel. About Locke's autobiography, *This World, My Home*, Adlai Stevenson wrote, "No one has told us what we are, who we are, and why we are as we are, with more grace and grandeur." Brooks Atkinson, *New York Times* drama critic, called the book "a social and spiritual history of America ... written by the only man who has the experience, the purity of character and the literary skill to render such an account of our national life."

If a journalist newly awakened to an outmoded land system was looking for a mentor, he could not have dreamed of one more fitting than Walter Locke. Locke's view of that issue is illustrated by the following excerpts from his account of the Seminole Indians. He was a teacher in Mekusukey, Oklahoma at a time when the

Seminoles, although confined to a reservation, ran their own affairs.

> Theirs was the one really free economy I have ever seen. Each man worked as pleased him, needing no other man's control. If some were more prosperous, others less, that merely reflected the difference in their skill and energy. Here all men were really born equal – equal in opportunity... The Seminole owned for himself whatever he made the land produce. The land itself he could not own. That, like the air and sun, was a common heritage. The nation owned the land...
>
> Each Seminole child had at its birth its free and equal access to the soil. It needed pay no man for a foothold on the earth on which, by no consent of its own, it had been cast... Since every man was free to make, on the soil, his own job, there could be no involuntary unemployment, no unwilling poverty. What was this but the Utopia of which, through the ages, men have dreamed?
>
> This Indian democracy was too simply good to survive the white man's greed... So this Indian nation, by act of Congress, was destroyed. There must be "free enterprise". The land was "allotted" as private property to the individual Indians. The white men then, in the old routine of beads and bottles, lured their land away from them...
>
> [*Years later, Locke returned and found out about the boys he had taught.*] Such as survived were hired laborers or living on relief. The Indian Eden of forty years before was becoming a smoking, disheveled, roaring white man's prosperity.

Locke also wrote about "makers of a world", prominent people he particularly admired – Walt Whitman, Jane Addams, Booker T. Washington, John Dewey, James M. Cox, Franklin Roosevelt, and Albert Einstein, among others. About George, Locke commented succinctly:

> Henry George was warning that back of all worldly problems lies the question of the land, man's common inheritance. That issue has been from his day to now overturning old world governments. Our day to face it cannot always be deferred.

Land as a Utility

Jean Lightfoot Kappell, a former *St. Louis Post* Washington correspondent, came to Dayton to marry a test pilot at Wright Patterson Air Force Base. After she wrote a brilliant letter to the editor about a foreign crisis, Locke set her to writing editorials instead of letters. Her insights made our editorial meetings exciting forays into environmental matters, cultural developments, and the causes and cures of the world's problems.

Jean had a novel approach to land and public finance. "Land value is a utility," she argued. People willingly pay according to how much electricity, water, or natural gas they are provided. To the extent they are provided with access to parks, schools, fire protection, roads, public transit – all the public amenities that affect the value of particular locations – they should find it just as reasonable to pay for their "land utilities", she maintained.

Filth and Wine

Observing that first impressions tend to be sharp and intense, Locke urged me to write an occasional column about the local scene, which I called "A Stranger Comes to Dayton". An early one caused a minor uproar.

On the "squawk box", the speaker booming live police radio calls into the newsroom, I heard an officer report, "We've got another suspect at Filth and Wine." That was cop jargon for the notorious Fifth and Wayne intersection. I explored and wrote about that dismal area. Among the many who called to complain the following day was the director of a branch bank. He was upset with me for running down his neighborhood, but he agreed when I asked if we could meet in his office.

I asked why he thought police dubbed a site two blocks away "Filth and Wine". He began telling me about conditions even worse than those I had described. He pointed out his window to apartments. "They've got outhouses in the back, no indoor toilets." He posed a thoughtful question: "What should be done? If inspectors close them down, where will poor renters live?"

Shortly afterwards I posed this question to Carl Feiss, a federal housing official who was attending a planning conference in town.

Instead of answering, he astonished me by saying Fifth and Wayne looks good compared to Hog Bottom, a Dayton neighborhood he had just toured. He called it "the worst slum on the American continent".

Could I quote him? Yes, he said, and we did, with photos of Hog Bottom's mud streets, shanties half falling down, and the poor blacks who lived there.

Dayton's congressman read the "worst slum" quote and went ballistic. Like many who were in denial about how the other half lived, he tried to get Feiss fired for "smearing" Dayton. Thankfully, he was unsuccessful.

Notwithstanding its slums, Dayton had many attractive neighborhoods, a lively downtown, vibrant industries and a clean city government. Equipment and paving salesmen would ask traffic engineer Tony Caruthers who they had to pay off to win contracts. When Caruthers said Dayton did not operate that way, they would plead in disbelief, "Come on Tony, how much?" Their insistence on trying to find someone to pay off was a sad commentary, revealing that bribery was the norm in many cities.

Land Speculation Trumps Enterprise

Locke, nearing 80, continued writing his column but gave up his editorial responsibilities. James E. Fain came from the Cox Atlanta papers as our new editor. He focused the paper's attention on the decay of central cities and the mushrooming of bedroom communities in former cornfields, a post-war phenomenon plaguing the nation.

To research some zoning practices and distorted growth patterns relating to this theme, I sought the perspectives of one of the area's major homebuilders.

"You're asking the wrong person," he said. "I shut down my housing operations." He said he had shifted into the "business", as he called it, of buying acreage around intersections of the newly launched Interstate Highway System.

The lure of land speculation had extinguished one of Dayton's useful enterprises and made its large cadre of managers and skilled workers search for other work. The former builder had found what appeared to be an easy way to siphon off location values created by America's new transportation network. He was avoiding the headaches and risks of building and selling homes. He anticipated it would be more profitable to buy key sites at low prices that he could sell later at much higher prices.

Eatin' Off It

Something discouraging was happening to Dayton's impressive business district. Buildings were being torn down for surface parking lots. Others looked shabby or were boarded up. The formerly compact skyline started to resemble a Hallowe'en pumpkin's grin with missing teeth.

I asked Henry Bader, the leading broker in downtown real estate, to share his views about this decline. Using his huge map of the central business district, he gave a memorable parcel-by-parcel narration of Dayton's development. He named the original owners of every lot on the major commercial streets and described the buildings they put up. He told which sons or grandsons rebuilt or modernized these structures up to a point several generations ago. Bader summed up his recitation of each parcel's history with a disheartening line: "That family's been eatin' off it ever since."

Out of scores of central city businesses, Rike's, the largest department store, a dress shop and a furniture store were the only three whose owners actually ran the businesses. The rest, Bader said, were being milked by absentee landlords, "eatin' off" their properties.

To verify his sorry tale, he sent me to talk to the head of Elders & Johnson, the second largest department store. Its president told me his fading company sent out rental checks to some ninety heirs of the original owners. These current owners, he said, ranged "from minor children to senile oldsters" who had addresses from California to the French Riviera. For decades these titleholders denied management requests to invest in modernization. Echoing Bader, the president said his multiple landlords were concerned only with their monthly checks, not the health of the enterprise. The fate of Dayton's economy, he said, was the farthest thing from their thinking.

A six-story building one block from the city's most valuable real estate was entirely vacant except for a top floor apartment occupied by the owners, two elderly sisters. Years earlier, after their property assessment was increased substantially, the sisters evicted their commercial and residential tenants and successfully challenged their assessment, winning lower taxes on the basis that their property was yielding no income. If the assessment had been based primarily on the site value, instead of largely on the building as is typical throughout America, this waste of a good structure and a prime location would not have occurred.

Like New York, Like Dayton

Albert Pleydell, a former assistant to New York's famed Mayor Fiorello LaGuardia, conducted research revealing that New York's property tax promoted blight. His critics said the nation's largest city was so unique and complex that no generalizations could be drawn from the study's findings. The Lincoln Foundation (which later formed the Lincoln Institute of Land Policy) asked Pleydell to study a more typical city. Dayton officials and civic leaders succeeded in inviting him there. "Taxation and Urban Blight: A Case Study of Greater Dayton"[2] revealed that Dayton's injurious property tax practices closely mirrored those in New York.

One would expect the value of buildings in nice residential and commercial sectors to be high relative to the value of their sites, and low in sectors with dilapidated housing or shops. Pleydell researched over 18,000 parcels, paired between Dayton's blighted sectors and control areas and matched for age of structures. In Dayton, as in New York, he found that the ratio of building to land values was almost identical throughout the city. This would seem to indicate either that the entire city was blighted, or that it was completely free of blight, neither of which was true. How to explain this incongruity?

The study revealed that assessors were systematically writing down the value of land in slum areas. They erroneously assumed that, because the *structures* were nearly worthless, the *land* under them also must be worth little. Had assessors paid attention to actual sales of these sites, or the income streams they produced, they would have discovered that many slum sites were far from cheap. Actually, the low assessments kept taxes low, making the slums profitable and highly prized, boosting their location values.

Property tax laws in Ohio, as in most states, require both land and improvements to be assessed according to market value. However, the study found that this law was disregarded. According to extensive actual sales data of both types of property, vacant sites were assessed far below market value, while new buildings were assessed far higher.

This explains why public agencies charged with carrying out slum clearance were often shocked at the high prices they had to pay to acquire these under-assessed sites. To fulfill their promises to provide low-priced housing for evicted slum dwellers, they needed to provide big unanticipated subsidies to buy out the slumlords.

Slumlords meanwhile could pack in renters and provide minimal repairs, then watch the value of their holdings rise as population growth increased the demand for housing. Moreover, the owners won lower taxes as the condition of their buildings worsened. Conscientious owners who upgraded their rental units, on the other hand, got higher assessments and higher taxes for their good behavior.

Is it any wonder, with such misuse of incentives, that blight was spreading in Dayton and in cities all across the country?

Redlining and Block-Busting

I met Erika Schulhof, an elementary teacher, shortly before she was due to leave for a job in California. She was born in Austria and sent by her parents at age 10 to Scotland on a Kindertransport before they were murdered by Nazis. She spent ten years in Scottish boarding schools before joining an aunt and uncle who had escaped to Ohio. To keep Erika in Dayton – and with me – I married her, and this talented and good human being became a wonderful wife, wonderful mother, and wonderful friend.

We got an education when we went house hunting. A realtor looked over our list of ads that looked interesting and affordable to us. He immediately crossed off several because "those will go black in a couple years". How did he know? The practice was called redlining. Realtors drew boundaries around areas where they decided blacks could live or move to. Whites like us were ushered not very subtly to other sectors. Within these redlined areas, mortgages and loans for home improvements, if available at all, could be obtained only on extremely unfavorable terms.

Block-busting was a nasty companion of redlining. Realtors would bring a black family into a neighborhood, and then use scare tactics to get whites to flee. This created the mistaken but widespread belief that property values would inevitably fall if minority residents moved into formerly all-white areas. Realtors and other investors then bought the properties on the cheap and sold them at inflated prices to blacks who had limited choices about where they could buy.

Federal policies at the time intensified both racial and economic segregation. To qualify for urban loans and grants, developers of new neighborhoods had to observe federal rules requiring uniform housing types that catered to households within a narrow economic stratum and that served a uniform racial population. In new sub-divisions this killed the diversity that once typified American neighborhoods. Cities are challenged to find their way back to a healthy mix of people and housing types.

My wife and I became active in a group that was promoting integrated neighborhoods. On a radio talk show I joined Charles Washington, head of the local Urban League, to discuss open housing, a policy to end housing discrimination and segregation. Charles was speaking eloquently about democratic ideals and equal housing opportunities when a caller interrupted:

"Mr Washington, that sounds fine, but how would you like to have Negroes move next to you?" Without mentioning that he was black, Charles Washington told her, "As a matter of fact, ma'am, Negro families live right next door to me and, honestly, I couldn't ask for nicer neighbors." We exchanged winks.

Citizens vs the Power Structure

My column broke the news that Dayton's small nature museum was about to be torn down for a parking lot. City Council in its wisdom decided this was a better use of the space. Contrary to the cliché that "you can't fight city hall", what ensued is a useful reminder to those who are engaged in social change that, indeed, citizens can prevail over a community's big decision makers.

The museum was run by part-time curator E.J. "Joe" Koestner, a high school biology teacher. It had stuffed birds, an Egyptian mummy, live native mammals and snakes, and an extensive fossil collection. People who were outraged by the city's decision to close it down asked Joe and me to try to save the museum. We met with the head of Dayton's industrial-commercial-political power structure that ran a kind of shadow government. He was cordial but said a museum project could not be put on the agenda because it would conflict with higher priorities that had already been set.

Some pro-museum folks with a company-town mentality said a "no" from a spokesman for the National Cash Register, Frigidaire, Delco, and other top local firms meant the cause was lost. Others, however, approved Koestner's unusual plan to stimulate support by holding backyard fairs. Koestner would bring along live raccoons, snakes, and hawks, teach about the animals in a hands-on way, and then collect nickels and dimes from the fascinated children and their parents. Interest mounted, civic groups contributed, and supporters formed the Dayton Natural History Society.

The city did tear down the museum but fended off criticism by offering a lovely city-owned wooded site – provided our society could finance a new museum. The power structure moved to squelch our fund-raising campaign but refrained when the heads of Dayton Power & Light and of Rike's department store broke ranks. Both of them declared that their life-long enjoyment of nature had been sparked by boyhood visits to the museum and they were eager to bring it back to life.

Never discount the role of luck. We envisioned a museum that portrayed how early life forms evolved into Ohio's present plants and creatures. We wanted visitors to see junior naturalists caring for animals and preparing exhibits. We wanted a museum that would increase conservation awareness among people in our region. The young architect we could afford realized he was falling short of these ambitious goals and generously put us in touch with his teacher, the famed Vienna-born Richard Neutra. It turned out that Neutra had always wanted to design a nature museum. We let him.

Hard-working museum supporters, armed with Neutra's splendid design, began to see funds pouring in. Patrons of the Dayton Art Institute, symphony, Junior League, city ballet, and others generously supported the project, putting to rest the power structure's fears that Dayton's cultural cup, so to speak, was filled to capacity. Ordinary citizens prevailed and the new museum, with Joe Koestner as full-time director, quickly began enriching the community as it taught environmental science to thousands, created popular summer courses, and led nearby archaeological digs.

The lesson relating to the larger theme of this book – overhauling our tax system and land policy – is that one *can* fight city hall and that social reform also needs to engender the kind of grass roots support and passion that gave birth to Dayton's nature museum.

Green Revolutionary

We got to know Mildred Loomis who ran the School of Living on Lane's End Farm near Dayton. A scholar and activist, she was a disciple of sociologist Ralph Borsodi whose 1929 book, *This Ugly Civilization*,[3] revealed his prescience about the boom conditions leading to the Great Depression.

Mildred and her followers promoted reforms in so many aspects of modern life, economic justice among them, that it boggled the mind. She and her husband John grew much of what they ate and made much of what they used. School members in New England created a currency that, unlike the dollar, retained a constant value. One of her associates, Robert Swann, founded the modern land trust movement. Her workshops, "Green Revolution" newsletter, and conferences influenced a wide circle of creative thinkers, Hazel Henderson, E.F. Schumacher of *Small Is Beautiful* fame, Scott Nearing, and J.I. Rodale, *Prevention* publisher and organic farming guru, to name a few.

Mildred opposed the rush toward bigness – corporate mergers, centralized political power, schools as educational factories, media cannibalizing, concentrated ownership of resources – as inimical to a free and humane society.

Already known as the "grandmother of the Green Revolution", Mildred naturally was thrilled in the spring of 1969 to see a headline in the *Baltimore Sun*: "Green Revolution to Feed Starving Millions". The article told of a biologist, Norman Borlaug, who developed strains of high-yielding wheat and rice that could mean "new life to the starving" in India and the Far East. As the article went on to explain that the plan required thousand-acre fields and tons of chemical fertilizers, Mildred was downhearted. She protested to the U.S. Department of Agriculture for supporting this "travesty" and misuse of her thirty-year-old slogan. USDA did not reply. She felt vindicated five years later when the department reported to the press that its so-called green revolution was a mistake. Large-scale mono-crop agriculture spread disease that was wiping out a whole season's crop and threatening worldwide starvation. Mildred remained convinced that small-scale organic farming was the wave of the future. She concluded her tale of this episode in her book, *Decentralism*,[4] by writing in bold type, "**Long live the Green Revolution!**"

The School of Living promoted wholesome natural foods. Some of their claims went off the deep end. Medical professionals, who should have been probing for facts and offering guidance, instead ridiculed Loomis and others in the budding nutrition movement as "food faddists". Similarly, when amateur land tax reformers in her camp made bizarre claims, economists largely derided their concerns instead of offering correctives to the genuine and serious problems these nonprofessionals detected.

Whose Moon?

Fellow editorial writer Jean Kappell was a gourmet cook as well as a keen political analyst, so a dinner invitation from her was always a delight. One time Jean, her husband Lon and their three-year-old daughter Taffy came out of their home to greet us. At the moment we arrived, a spectacular moon was just rising above the horizon, one of those gigantic moons that seem close enough to touch.

Taffy cried out, "Mommy, I want that moon"

"You know why you can't have it, dear?" Jean asked tenderly.

With a big smile the toddler replied, " 'Cause it's everybody's moon."

Out of the mouths of babes. Or, more accurately, out of the mouths of a babe whose mother taught her early and well. Everybody's moon. Everybody's earth.

NOTES

1. Antioch Press, Yellow Springs, Ohio, 1957.
2. Tax Study Advisory Committee, Dayton, Ohio, 1982.
3. Reprinted by Porcupine Press, 1972.
4. School of Living Press, York, Pa., 1980.

16

Washington Assignment

LEAVING DAYTON friends and activities was wrenching for my family. It underscored our awareness that smaller communities are national treasures endowed with special and often underappreciated virtues and qualities.

The separation ache eased, however, when it became clear that serving as Washington Bureau Chief for Cox Newspapers was a journalist's dream job.

Was it work or play to cover the nation's capital? It involved catching history-making Senate and House debates, questioning legislators, chatting with White House staff, participating in presidential press conferences, roaming the State Department and endless Pentagon halls to track movements toward war or peace, hearing intricate Supreme Court cases, finding the human touch or comic situation amid streams of serious stuff, and stopping at the National Gallery of Art between the Capitol and my office to meditate in a chamber full of Rembrandts.

Gourmet snacks at embassy affairs also came with the job. Simeon Booker, chief of Johnson Publications in the office next to mine, was constantly invited to embassy military events because foreign diplomats thought that *Jet*, Johnson's news magazine for and about Afro-Americans, was all about airplanes.

Washington reporters can too easily acquire a sense of self-importance as national and world leaders treat them with great deference. This is heady stuff, making it easy to forget why people of high rank are uncommonly nice to journalists. Simply put, getting good press is essential to the careers and reputations of top officials and other prominent men and women.

Civil Rights – a Broken Congress?

My arrival in Washington coincided with the most intensive effort to erase laws and practices that consigned people of color to second class citizenship. President Kennedy's comprehensive proposals addressed critical issues: guaranteeing and enforcing the right to vote; halting discrimination in restaurants and other public places; overcoming barriers to school desegregation; and assuring equal job opportunities.

Knowing now how this all turned out, it is difficult to recapture the nation's mood of uncertainty over the outcome of that struggle to enact civil rights laws. Walter Lippmann, the era's most prestigious columnist, felt during those legislative battles that Congress was moving so painfully slowly that he proposed switching to the British parliamentary system. Many observers concurred and my editors occasionally questioned why I had a contrary view.

Fresh on the scene, it struck me that part of the genius of the congressional machinery was that it *did* allow time. Time for Southern senators to let off steam during a filibuster. Time for Southern voters to hear the majority's eagerness for reform. Time for the clergy, belatedly, to declare civil rights a moral issue. Time for Southern voices, Ralph McGill of our Atlanta paper prominently among them, to come out of the woodwork and call for an end to Jim Crow. And time to let opponents win minor skirmishes en route to defeat. Thus, when civil rights victories finally came, passions had subsided, no secession or civil war was threatened, and progress gained a momentum that would prove impossible to roll back.

My respect for the process was reinforced by contact with an unsung civil rights hero, Congressman William M. McCulloch, a conservative Republican from Piqua, Ohio, a little town north of Dayton.[1] Unlike flamboyant colleagues, Bill was self-effacing in his rise to become ranking minority member of the House Judiciary Committee. Before the full House, when he said so quietly and earnestly that it was downright un-American to deny equal rights, the chamber hushed. This won him no popular acclaim in his all-white district, where he suffered many unkind attacks for championing minority rights.

McCulloch's stature among Republicans enabled him to bring his party into harmony with a bill proposed by a Democratic president and a Democratic-controlled Congress. No small matter, that. To counter their Southern bloc, the Democratic White House and Justice Department could not win without Republican votes. McCulloch persuaded Senate Minority Leader Everett Dirksen, long tepid on civil rights, to support compromises that brought the bulk of the GOP into the proponents' camp.[2] Whenever the bill's chances looked grim, McCulloch reassured me that behind-the-scenes bipartisan maneuvers were forging a winning strategy.

UNLIKELY FEMINIST

A delicious sidelight of the legislative civil rights tug-of-war was that Virginia Democratic Congressman Howard "Judge" Smith, powerful chair of the House Rules Committee, became an inadvertent women's champion. Cynically aiming to attract enough opposition to kill the civil rights bill, he inserted an amendment prohibiting discrimination on the basis of sex. To Smith's consternation, and the delight of women's rights groups, his amendment passed along with the rest of the bill.

Land Issue Not Cooking

How long would it be, I wondered, before our slow legislative machinery set aright America's unjust land tenure system, as it had done in the civil rights field. A clue that land was not even on the back burner came during a press conference. Walter Heller, chief White House economist, was describing the dangers of inflation as he pointed to rising prices of TVs, radios, food, and other goods. I asked if he was looking at how land price escalation was fueling the inflation of housing, food, and manufactured items.

"I don't follow you," Heller said with a puzzled look.

Dick Stroud of the *Christian Science Monitor* spoke up for me. "You know, land prices are really soaring and foreigners are buying lots of farmland, bidding up acreage prices. Is there something that should be done about this?"

Reporters rolled their eyes when Heller responded, "If it's such a good investment, I guess the federal government should buy land."

Despite his blind spot in land policy, so common among economists, Heller was an eminent authority on federal taxation. In the 1940s, policies he designed for West Germany spurred its post-war recovery. When President Johnson refused Heller's advice to raise taxes to finance the Vietnam War and avoid putting the nation on a path toward steep inflation, Heller admirably followed his conscience and resigned his prestigious White House job.

Right and Left

The land issue was not completely hidden. A leading conservative, Republican Congressman Thomas B. Curtis of Missouri, and a leading liberal, Democrat Senator Edmund Muskie of Maine, both spoke about features of the property tax that were tearing apart the fabric of our cities.

Representative Curtis called the hoarding of strategically located lands "the greatest of all economic sins". His corrective: "A well-designed real estate tax system places an incentive on utilizing real estate to its greatest economic potential"[3] He lamented that scholars for twenty-five years had neglected the property tax, which he dubbed the Cinderella of revenue devices.

Senator Muskie, a member of the Advisory Commission on Intergovernmental Relations (ACIR), called on state legislators to update assessments that lagged by years or decades, to obey laws requiring assessment uniformity, and to eliminate favored treatment of wealthy neighborhoods.[4] Research reports by the highly competent ACIR staff – Laszlo Ecker-Ratz, John Shannon, William Colman, and other fiscal experts – provided a rich lode of information for easing state and local problems.

Few journalists joined in mining this ACIR source. Beside myself, to my knowledge only Harlan Trott of the *Christian Science Monitor*, Richard Noyes, editor of the *Salem (NH) Observer*, Will Lissner of the *New York Times*, who was also the founder-editor of the *American Journal of Economics and Sociology*, and Perry Prentice, *Time* vice president and *House and Home* editor, were reporting ACIR's evidence of the detrimental effects of local tax systems.

The Reagan administration, despite its rhetoric about excessive federal power, incongruously disbanded ACIR which, more than any other agency, was devising specific guidelines for restoring state and local powers.

Looting in Broad Daylight

When President Lyndon Johnson's War on Poverty was being launched, Martin Luther King, Jr, testified about the immorality of dire poverty amidst great wealth. He cited *Progress and Poverty* but legislators did not pursue Henry George's program for overcoming this disparity.[5] After King was assassinated, riots broke out in over one hundred cities. People looted merchandise from shops in broad daylight. People were shocked.

I could not help thinking that day in and day out, year in and year out, owners of prime real estate were engaging in the whole-sale looting of the earnings of residents and businesses. This takes place with the full support of the law and with the tacit approval of most officials and citizens. Few appear shocked that a very small minority skims off wealth that belongs to everyone. Both types of looting bear examination.

Heavy smoke, along with the sadness of King's murder, hung over the nation's capital. Cars heading out of the city jammed the streets. Sirens screamed. Fire engines threaded their way to trouble spots. Yet the riot scene took on a carnival aspect. Looters laughed, shouted, and ambled with armloads and shopping carts full of toys, lamps, clothes, linoleum rolls, and boxes of who knows what. Some commentators, acknowledging the understandable frustration of blacks, whose great leader and peacemaker had been cut down, came close to condoning the stealing and destruction. Only material things were involved, they said.

People come first, before things, in my view too, but drawing a moral boundary between human and material values struck a wrong chord. *People* built and worked in those shattered shops. *People* lived in the torched apartments. *People* labored to provide the pillaged inventories. *People* lost the livelihoods that went up in flames. *People* were condemned to live long after amidst scars of this destruction of *things*.

Another kind of looting lets landlords procure trillions of dollars worth of the people's wealth annually. The land rents they collect are created by the entire community, not by the landowners. This looting of the common wealth goes on in broad daylight and in the dark of night, in rain and in shine. Hallowed by tradition, it wears a cloak of respectability.

This morally indefensible activity lying at the very heart of our economy causes no end of damage. It infects business leaders, bankers, religious leaders, physicians, and officials in high office whose ethical lapses have become commonplace. The mass of citizens, without necessarily understanding that their common heritage is being looted, nevertheless sense that a climate of unfairness prevails. If they can be scandalized when Wall Street moguls deal themselves outsize bonuses, how much angrier will they be when they awaken to the more monumental robbery of their wages, their savings, and their fair portion of nature's bounty?

Treadmill Effects

In the 1950s and 1960s, politicians faced an array of socio-economic problems that could no longer be swept under the rug. They pledged to halt joblessness, crime, failing schools, miserable housing, clogged highways, decaying cities, and urban sprawl. They declared wars on drugs and poverty. They created new organizations including departments of Housing and Urban Development, Transportation, and Health, Education and Welfare; the Appalachian Regional Commission, and the Environmental Protection Agency. New programs included Revenue Sharing, Head Start, Block Grants, and Model Cities. These all stemmed from attempts during the Kennedy, Johnson, Nixon, and Carter years to find federal remedies.

Other nonprofit, state, and local programs that came on the scene to attack these problems included public-private partnerships, Habitat for Humanity, privatization (even of garbage disposal, school operations, and prisons), Enterprise Zones, tax base sharing, metropolitan governance, tax abatements, farmland tax exemptions, new towns, conservation easements, and transferable development rights, to make only a partial list.

Most of these efforts earned an A-plus for effort but a D-minus for results. To justify the billions expended, administrators pointed to affordable homes built, delinquents rehabilitated, skyscrapers replacing slums, fragile habitats saved, and so forth.

Looking at national and local trends, however, these remedies encountered what I call a *treadmill effect*. Programs had to run faster and faster as the problems multiplied. Blight outpaced urban renewal. Crime and drug-dealing outpaced imprisonment and mentoring. Dumb growth trumped smart growth. For lack of accurate diagnoses, most efforts treated symptoms. Untouched root causes continued to do their damage.[6]

I part company with those who blame these failures on bureaucrats. Our anonymous army of public servants impressed me as conscientious, far outperforming their reputation. It seemed patently unfair to fault them for carrying out laws designed by academic experts, private consultants, lobbyists for special interests, and legislators. Even laws and programs that appear on target often have built-in loopholes that almost preordain that they will fail.

Offering Alternatives

When I queried people in government about land-related solutions to problems they were trying to address, it was not uncommon to get blank looks as if I were talking in some Martian lingo. Ironically, public leaders who, in their official capacities, pleaded ignorance about the existence of land speculation would, at social gatherings, be heard bragging about their latest killings from land deals.

So I took another tack. My burgeoning collection of articles, speeches, and research findings about the need to modernize land policies had grown into a four-inch-thick volume. An assistant secretary of the Department of Housing and Urban Development (HUD), formed to save cities, agreed to review it.[7]

After several months of no response, I told Richard Goodwin, the White House domestic affairs specialist, about my collection. He asked why land tax reform was not on the front burner if it was half as important as I was claiming. I suggested that economists who were aware of the perverse incentives eroding the economy were keeping quiet, but should be shouting from the rooftops that a land tax would reduce land prices, create jobs, and save cities.

Goodwin did not give me a blank look. Within a short time, he alerted me that White House aide Bill Moyers and Robert C. Weaver, Secretary of HUD, would hold a press conference about the formation of a presidential urban commission. Clever politician, Goodwin let me assume this was "my baby", a notion reinforced in my mind when Moyers said the commission would be charged to "discover ways of making the real estate tax structure more viable", and when Weaver said the commission would confront "really sticky problems" affecting housing such as "the taxation thing". Asked to elaborate, Weaver said, "If we simply tax the land and not the improvement on the land, as they do in Australia, many think this should be helpful."

As I learned later, my input was only one of many. Several prominent urbanologists had spread alarm that the nation's cities were in a tailspin and urged the White House to halt it. Though the commission may have had only a little of my DNA in its origins, it changed the course of my career.

Notes

1. McCulloch later was recognized for his pivotal role when Dayton Congressman Charles Whalen and his wife Barbara authored *The Longest Debate*, Seven Locks Press, Washington, D.C., 1985.
2. As the debate wound down, the Senate chamber and press gallery were almost empty when Illinois Democrat Paul H. Douglas, an early civil rights champion, urged passage. When Dirksen, a recent convert to the cause, gave concluding arguments, crowds of reporters and cheering senators were on hand. I wrote about this ironic twist and Robert Gruenberg of the *Chicago Daily News* sent my article to Douglas. Douglas wrote me a thank-you note saying that, having been a football lineman in college, he was used to seeing the quarterbacks get all the glory.
3. Congressional Record, 8/10/65, p.A4227.
4. Address to the American Assembly, Arden House, Harriman, NY, 1966.
5. After Rev. King met with the President, our Cox bureau staff met King with a taxi to take him to lunch. As we drove out the White House grounds, we noticed skinheads carrying mean-spirited posters denouncing King. The driver turned to King and said, "I'd like to sock them in the jaw." The famous pacifist smiled and said, "That's not exactly my style."
6. The War on Poverty's emphasis on schooling to reduce unemployment was a case in point. My critical elaboration on that theme, "Education Alone Could Fail", is summarized in Appendix A.
7. Appendix B, with samples of my collection, reveals that a significant amount of work on the topic was available. This body of knowledge was a kind of elephant in the room that most officials and academics managed to ignore.

17

The Douglas Commission

"WOULD YOU LIKE TO BE MY ASSISTANT?"

That was the last thing I expected to hear when I was interviewing Paul H. Douglas about his plans after President Johnson named him head of the newly created National Commission on Urban Problems. Switching from journalism to economics was no small matter, yet such was my admiration for Douglas that I did not hesitate to give him an enthusiastic "*Yes!*"

Douglas was known as "the conscience of the Senate" and also as "a winner of lost causes". A former University of Chicago economics professor, Douglas added new dimensions to economic theory. Though exempt from military service at age 50, he volunteered for the Marines in World War II and sustained battle wounds that left him permanently disabled. After eighteen years as an Illinois senator, he was defeated by Charles Percy in 1966. Early in that campaign Percy's daughter was assassinated. As the crime went unsolved, Douglas ordered his team to say nothing against his opponent. Also, Douglas's campaign leaders urged him not to discuss race issues because of a white backlash against civil rights protests in Illinois at that time. Disregarding their advice, Douglas began every campaign speech by calling on people of all colors to learn to live together in harmony.

The commission was charged to recommend ways to improve housing and building codes, federal and local taxes, development standards, technical innovations, and industry practices "to prevent slums, blight and sprawl, preserve natural beauty, and provide for a decent home and suitable living environment for every American family".

During our first month Douglas led commission members and staff through high-level bull sessions.[1] He challenged us, asking: "What can we do to justify the million-dollars we've been given?" We identified some forty research projects to be undertaken by staff and outside specialists. Experts, Douglas cautioned, "should be on tap, not on top". To avoid an ivory tower approach, he insisted that members and staff visit cities around the country to rub our noses in the problems we would be investigating and trying to find solutions for.

We moved into modest offices three blocks from the White House. Mr D, as staff called Douglas, began hanging pictures of people he most admired – lawyer Clarence Darrow, Illinois Governor John Altgeld, and Hull House founder Jane Addams, all champions of the underdog. Marching with another picture into my office he said, "Here's one that should be looking over your shoulder." Henry George! Neither of us had mentioned that name to each other, so I said it must take a Georgist to recognize one. He laughed, saying he had long been convinced that land problems were at the heart of city problems.

Vox Populi

It fell to me to set up study tours and hearings. Our first outing to Baltimore illustrates why this task was a breeze. No sooner had I mentioned Douglas to Republican Mayor Theodore McKeldin than he said, "I love that man, one of our greatest senators ever." He offered to do whatever we requested to make the Commission visit a success. Two days before our due date, a McKeldin aide phoned to assure me that our several meeting places were ready. He added what the mayor surely did not want him to say: "Our street cleaning and trash people are out in force, cleaning up the places around there." A former Chicago alderman, Douglas knew these tricks. After official tours, we made it a point to visit the seedier parts of cities on our own.

Some 350 local officials, urban specialists, academics, builders, developers and citizens in thirty cities shared their ideas and complaints with us. We heard two common but contradictory themes: one, tell the feds to get out of our hair so we can run our own show;

two, tell the feds we desperately need more money and more help
to solve our problems. Poor whites, blacks and Hispanics who
testified were remarkably articulate. They pinpointed community
problems with a directness and even eloquence that many professors, elected officials, and other professionals did not match.[2]

In pursuit of affordable housing, the commission pressed builders
to share, publicly or in private, detailed data about their costs and
earnings. We learned that many successful developers barely broke
even from sales of the actual houses they constructed, but profited
mainly from the land appreciation that occurred between the time
they bought and sold. "Land banking" was a typical builder practice. They had to become temporary land speculators to avoid
having other long-term speculators take all the profits out of their
projects. James Rouse, creator of Columbia, would not share his
land cost data for the 14,000 acres – one-tenth of Maryland's rural
Howard County – needed for his model new town between Baltimore and Washington. We knew that to keep his land costs down
he employed a mini-army of brokers to secretly acquire the sites
without revealing the buyer or his plans.

New Orleans officials complained to the Commission that
federal guidelines for housing grants and loans were set too low for
their city's unusually high land costs. How much, Douglas asked,
are you taxing land? New Orleans was taking in less revenue from
property taxes than from sales taxes. Property taxes were so low,
we learned, because the position of assessor in every parish of the
city was handed down from fathers to sons or nephews whose
implicit duty was to disregard market values and keep assessments
low. Any competent land economist could have told New Orleans
what Douglas's question implied: that their abnormally high real
estate costs were inevitable under this regimen of low land taxes.

A Lesson in Taking Criticism

"You call it urban renewal. We call it Negro removal." Angry black
citizens at New Haven hearings attacked a program that Douglas,
as senator, had helped steer through Congress. Legislators whose
fingerprints are all over a major federal program typically defend
that program to the death. Not Douglas. He was man enough to
say urban renewal was not working out as he had anticipated, and
he joined in the criticism.

HUD and the White House, unwilling to re-examine a program in which they had invested heavily, took umbrage. HUD sent a man we called the department's "spy" to our open sessions. The White House even tried to undermine our work by creating a new competing group.[3]

When Douglas went to the White House to present the Commission's final report to Johnson, the President snubbed him, kept him waiting long after the pre-arranged appointment, and then sent an assistant, Joseph Califano, in his stead.[4]

When urban renewal was new, it was the topic of an editorial writers' conference I attended in Philadelphia. Noted planner Edmund Bacon used a medical analogy to explain the concept. Slums and blight are cancerous, so bulldozing them and replacing them with attractive buildings will encourage healthy growth around previously sick places, Bacon asserted.

As wrecking balls cleared slums across the nation, Jane Jacobs, a keen observer of cities and writer (author of *The Death and Life of Great American Cities*, 1961), raised alarms. The demolished apartments and shops, she noted, often were vibrant neighborhoods with valuable webs of personal relationships and commercial services. She called the modern buildings that replaced them sterile places that people could not wait to flee after their 9-to-5 workdays.

Beyond these sociological impacts, poorly understood economic factors doomed the renewal program. Rejuvenation did not occur around renewed areas in Philadelphia or elsewhere. Adjacent owners saw slumlords bailed out at handsome prices and figured the feds would bail them out too if they let their buildings run down. Blight, instead of being contained, spread. Wasteland surrounded fine showplace buildings in Atlanta, Detroit, and other cities. New Haven kept enlarging its blight removal sectors until, by the time of our hearings, virtually the entire city had been designated an urban renewal area. Understandably, displaced people with nowhere they could afford to go vented their anger to us.

Focus on Land

Alan D. Manvel, associate director of the Commission and the former head of the Census of Governments, completed groundbreaking research reports.[5] One measured the dimensions of the escalation of land values from 1956 to 1966. Among the findings:

- The value of all taxable real estate (land and structures combined) increased *90 percent* during the decade, from $697 billion to $1.262 trillion.
- The value of land alone increased *95 percent*, from $269 billion to $523 billion.
- Increases in land value varied by property type – farm acreage, *81 percent*; industrial sites, *90 percent*; commercial land, *93 percent*; single-family sites, *106 percent*; vacant lots, *109 percent*; and multi-family sites, *141 percent*.

This dramatic doubling of land values during one decade was a prelude to even steeper increases in the 1980s and then the massive bubble that burst in 2007. Data showed that central city officials who bemoaned their "declining tax bases" were mistaken. They reacted to the fact that property tax bills on *housing* clearly were about as high as voters would tolerate. Yet if officials had reduced taxes on voters' houses and business structures and shifted the tax burden onto *land values*, cities could have tapped into this bonanza that was literally under their feet.

Another Manvel study disclosed the surprisingly large numbers of vacant in-city sites. A common complaint of city planners and officials is that cities have little space for development. This view was exploded by a survey of 106 large cities. On average, in cities of 100,000 people and over, *22 percent* of privately owned developable sites were vacant. In cities of 250,000 and over, *13 percent* were vacant. And these figures counted only completely undeveloped sites, not parcels on which obsolete structures made them ripe for redevelopment. Some cities had far more vacant sites – 49 percent in Phoenix, 54 percent in San Diego, 68 percent in Beaumont, Texas.

Given the steady exodus of people and companies from central cities to suburbs, undeveloped and under-developed sites are even more numerous today. With the proper strategy, this space constitutes a potential new frontier capable of giving new life to cities.

Taxes that are too high on buildings and too low on sites combine to drive growth out of cities. High building taxes discourage development. Low land taxes drive up land costs. Together, overtaxing structures and undertaxing land values effectively hamper the use of cities' sizeable inventory of sites that are vacant or that contain structures long overdue for replacement.

Mayor Tom L. Johnson, Cleveland's mayor in the early 1900s, understood this. What made him such a formidable foe of land monopolists was that he had been a former monopolist himself and knew the tricks of the trade, so to speak. He said:

> So long as it is permitted to take nature's resources that do not belong to them, plenty men of my kind will be ready to jump in and do the stealing. My mission is to take what people are stupid enough to let me take, and to show them how they can end the system that enriches me and impoverishes them.

Measure of a Man

The final Commission report, *Building the American City*,[6] attacked redlining, block-busting, exclusionary zoning, and other practices and laws that perpetuated housing segregation and discrimination. It offered nearly one hundred recommendations addressed to the various levels of government on housing costs, orderly land use, development standards, urban governance and finance, and on conserving the environment. Many proposals found their way into federal, state, and local laws. Others remain as unfinished business, worthy guides for urban officials looking for answers.

Douglas himself penned a hard-hitting section on taxing land, urging the public to recoup the huge value increases the commission had documented. Rare for a commission chair, Douglas worked tirelessly in writing major portions of the report, which makes the following incident particularly poignant.

The day came to release our recommendations to the public. Howard Shuman, the Commission's capable executive director, joined me early in the morning at Mr D's office to prepare for a noon press conference. But Douglas had something else on his mind: "What's going to happen now to my staff?"

We gave him a rundown of the plans of every professional and secretary. Some were returning to former positions and others were joining professional organizations, teaching, and so forth. At the bottom of the totem pole, however, was Willie, our odd-jobs aide. We said he had lined up a job at the Labor Department but just got "bumped" by someone with a veteran's preference.

Douglas – despite his White House snub, the HUD opposition and "spy", the culmination of two years of work, and the few hours till our press conference – said more forcefully than usual, "I don't want you to do another thing until you find a job for Willie."

Moved by Mr D's sense of priorities, we did make dozens of calls and successfully landed Willie a job that very morning.

Douglas was noted more for his liberal views on social issues than for his equally conservative views on fiscal matters. Perhaps what most made him stand out from the crowd, however, was the complete integration of his actions with his philosophy of putting people first and underdogs foremost.

NOTES

1. Once when some far-out ideas were being voiced, Commission member David Baker said, "Whoa. They won't let me back in Orange County [California] with my name on proposals like those. Back home folks are so conservative, if they take LSD, all they see is Lawrence Welk." (LSD was a mind-changing drug of that era and Welk's music was a bubbly style favored by oldsters.)
2. Published testimony, including question-and-answer sessions, are a treasure trove of commentary on many facets of urban life and governance. *Hearings Before the National Commission on Urban Problems*, Vols 1-5, Government Printing Office, Library of Congress No. 68-60024, Washington, D.C., 1968. See Appendix C for excerpts from the hearings transcripts.
3. The President's Committee on Urban Housing, headed by Edgar Kaiser, borrowed heavily from previous studies.
4. This insulting behavior was puzzling. Douglas had labored mightily to present a package of useful guidelines for the administration. Moreover, he was one of the few prominent elected leaders who stood by Johnson on Vietnam after most had come to feel the Administration's war policy was a disaster.
5. Alan D. Manvel, "Trends in the Value of Real Estate and Land, 1956 to 1966" and "Land Use in 106 Large Cities", in *Three Land Research Studies*, National Commission on Urban Problems, Government Printing Office, Washington, D.C., 1968.
6. Frederick A. Praeger, New York, 1969.

18

A Capital Idea

TOURISTS IN THE NATION'S CAPITAL get a rush of patriotism from the famous monuments, iconic buildings, cherry blossoms in spring, and debates in the chambers of Congress, where they may see a bit of democracy in action.

Few visitors, however, see the things that make Washington all too similar to other large cities: the homeless and jobless, the boarded-up apartments and abandoned shops, or the drug addicts, criminals, and mentally broken people. Many visitors are unaware that District of Columbia residents suffer from one of the causes of the Revolution, taxation without representation, because they are without voting legislators in the House or Senate where federal taxes are enacted.

Potential Model

What a marvel it would be if Washington, D.C. became a national model, demonstrating how a city can achieve prosperity and equal opportunity for all.

A small step toward this lofty goal presented itself in 1974 when Congress gave the District limited home rule, allowing it to elect its mayor and city council.[1]

Since the District government would soon be imposing local taxes (subject to Congressional review), the Tax and Revenue Committee of the appointive Council held hearings to design the city's revenue system. Invited to testify on property taxes, I urged the District to adopt state-of-the-art practices to upgrade its tax management system:

- Annual reassessments to keep pace with the ups and downs of real estate values.
- Full market value assessments rather than fractional assessments that hide errors, confuse taxpayers, and make it difficult to compare one's assessments with those of neighbors.
- Simple and transparent appeals procedures as a check on assessing errors.
- Separate and careful assessments of land and improvements.

If the District wanted to be ahead of the curve in modernizing its property tax, I suggested further that it allow Council to shift tax burdens off improvements and on to community-created land values.

"How is that working out in Australia?" asked Tedson Meyers, the committee chair.

Only a knowledgeable follower of land taxation could ask such a question. Happily shocked, I realized I had an unanticipated ally. Meyers tossed softball questions to let me expound on how land value taxation in Australia avoids penalizing people who upgrade their homes, commercial structures, and neighborhoods. Meyers next persuaded a congressman to include language in the home rule measure, specifically permitting city council to establish "... *different tax rates for land and for improvements thereon.*"

This simple, concise wording would let Council increase tax rates on land and reduce them on improvements, or even lower the tax rate on improvements to zero. This provision, enacted as part of Public Law 93-407, was signed by President Nixon. This by no means implies that Nixon intended to open the door to permit land value taxation or was even aware of the above key phrase.

How did Meyers become a friend of tax reform? A prominent communications lawyer and one-time president of the prestigious Cosmos Club, he was stuck with a long layover in the Bogotá airport and picked up a copy of *Progress and Poverty*. As he read it, he recalled saying to himself, "Ah, so that's why the new buildings and economic growth we so desperately wanted in the District [in the 1960s] were popping up across the Potomac River in Virginia."[2]

Slick

The following year the District finally had elective officials. Tedson and I called on Marion Barry, an ex-science teacher and community activist who had replaced Meyers as Finance and Revenue Committee chair.[3] We told him that he could give homeowners and businesses big tax breaks and spur private renewal by down-taxing buildings and by raising taxes on sites, and that he could do all this without begging for federal aid.

"That's pretty slick," he responded, grasping the concept right away. Barry then revealed his political smarts by asking, "How many votes do you have to support me on this?" We admitted that most District citizens probably never heard of land taxation and thus could not be counted on to advocate it. Clearly a public education program would be needed to bring them up to speed.

A League of Our Own

Barry's query spurred Tedson and me to start that education effort. We formed the League for Urban Land Conservation with a cast drawn from a variety of backgrounds and expertise. Board members ranged from radical community activist Josephine Butler on the left to conservative businessman Jesse Zeeman on the right. The deep friendships and a sense of common purpose that motivated our diverse group illustrated that the concern for land justice cuts across and unites supposedly opposing ideologies.

The District was uniquely fortunate in that era to have top-flight economists in charge of its tax office. Revenue Director Kenneth Back and his assessment specialist, John Rackham, recognized the validity of land value taxation and fed the League supportive information. We initiated seminars for economists, planners, and businessmen, encouraging land tax opponents to speak out so we could deal with their viewpoints. We invited D.C. clergy to an excellent talk by Robert Andelson, Auburn University philosophy professor, a talk that was later expanded into his book, *From Wasteland to Promised Land*.[4]

The Metropolitan Board of Trade, the area's leading business group, gave us a respectful hearing and fairly summarized the land tax in its bulletin. Insiders informed us, however, that a spokesman for the powerful parking lot bloc called us communists at a board meeting and persuaded the Board to vigorously oppose any moves to implement the reform. The cause of their antagonism was not difficult to decipher. Parking lot operators' valuable empty lots used for car parks would no longer benefit from their ultra-low taxes and the jig would be up on their land speculation game.

The League carried out a detailed computer simulation to learn how District property tax burdens would change under a split-rate system, that is, with a lower tax rate on buildings than on land values. One important finding was that average homeowners would enjoy lower taxes. Another was that the greatest percentage reductions in tax bills would occur in the poorest neighborhoods. This revealed that the current property tax system overburdens poor areas and favors affluent neighborhoods.

Before Rackham left the D.C. government to become the top realty tax specialist with the U.S. Postal Service, he simulated the effects of a pure land tax – that is, with District homes and other structures totally exempt and with property tax revenues generated from land values only. His findings (Table 1) revealed that shifting taxes off buildings would greatly benefit most homeowners, apartment owners and owners of large commercial buildings.

TABLE 1

Changes in D.C. Property Tax Bills
If the Tax Were Based on Land Values Only
(All Buildings Exempt)

Property category	Average percentage change for properties in each category*
Vacant sites	134% higher
Single-family homes	18% lower
Row dwellings	14% lower
Semi-detached dwellings	21% lower
Elevator apartments	23% lower
Walk-up apartments	39% lower
Large office buildings	13% lower

* Assumes the city raises the same revenue from the land tax as from the current property tax.

In contrast, holders of vacant sites with no building tax reductions to counteract their increased land taxes would experience big tax increases. This would give them a jolt to put their idle holdings into use, one of the purposes of the land tax.

The League testified frequently at tax hearings, each time winning more people to its camp. Several Council members supported the reform but would suddenly become silent on the issue. They gave no reasons, but it was common knowledge that parking lot owners and other real estate interests were the biggest financial contributors to local election campaigns.

To offset the paucity of media coverage of League meetings and speakers, we published "Landmarks", an occasional newsletter, to circulate our message. When Metro proposed fare increases to ease the subway system's financial shortfalls, the League issued a pamphlet opposing fare hikes. Rather, it urged Metro to raise revenue from the "free riders", namely, the property owners around Metro stops who were co-opting Metro-created land values.

Irony of Homelessness

The plight of the homeless became a front-burner issue nationally and in D.C. Their advocates in the nation's capital protested, marched, fasted, and pulled publicity stunts to demand shelters, soup kitchens, and patrols to rescue street people in freezing weather. The League did not join or oppose these approaches but focused on policies that could house the homeless. We documented the fact that Washington had roughly 7,000 boarded-up housing units, more than enough to house the hordes of homeless. In addition, we counted some 10,000 privately owned vacant lots that could serve long-term housing needs.

It was unconscionable that men and families were sleeping in cars, on open-air heating grates, in doorways, and in abandoned buildings with no place to bathe or escape the rain, cold, and extreme heat while potential housing and home sites lay dormant.

Church leaders and others with social concerns agreed. Under League leadership they joined to form the Pro-Housing Property Tax Coalition. This action group promoted land taxation as a means of resurrecting dwellings held in cold storage. Pete Farina, an idealistic young man who lived in and managed a group house for poverty-stricken people, headed the coalition.

Unfortunately, Back and Rackham had both departed from the D.C. Tax and Revenue Department. Their replacements prepared misleading reports (to put it charitably) that homeowners would pay more under a land tax. Yet public pressure mounted for this reform. John Wilson, the Council's Taxation and Revenue chair, rejected the land tax remedy and proposed what looked like a facsimile – creation of a new real estate class comprised of unused properties that would be taxed at a higher rate than used properties.[5]

Our Coalition's warnings that this would be an administrative nightmare were ignored.

When this new vacant class went into effect, landlords instantly found ways around it. Owners of boarded-up housing claimed they were "just on the verge" of putting their units back on the market and did not owe the higher tax. To verify such claims would have taken an army of inspectors. Parking lot owners for their part convinced officials that their crumbled paving and two-bit shacks constituted "improvements", so they also escaped being classified as vacant and avoided the higher tax rate.

The city intermittently abandoned and revived its vacant property tax. This had no demonstrable impact on reducing the large inventory of idle properties. Yet Council balked at enacting a land tax that would have worked automatically – without enforcement complications – to put idle sites and structures back into use.

Washington was not unique. Homelessness and boarded-up housing existed side by side across the nation. How can a society that, on the whole, is more affluent and more comfortably housed than the world has ever known, permit this? Why are people not sufficiently scandalized to insist that a tested and ready-made solution be put into operation? Why do we tolerate the perpetuation of misery, joblessness, and homelessness when we have the financial wherewithal and the knowledge to substantially reduce such shameful conditions?

Speculators' Rule of Thumb

Idle lots and buildings puzzled people. How could owners afford to hold onto them when they yielded no income? Owners with low or moderate incomes clearly cannot afford to do so. It is a different story with those who have deep pockets. Only owners with more than enough income from other sources play this game. They use the speculators' rule of thumb: if your property's yearly increases in value are greater than your annual holding costs, you come out ahead. The holding costs are mainly the annual property taxes.

Parking lot owners in the heart of downtown face higher property taxes than landlords of blighted apartments or empty lots farther out. So they do need some income to pay those taxes while waiting to recoup the growing value of their holdings. Parking fees serve this purpose.

Owners of slums and surface car parks sit and wait, wasting a community's most valuable resource, its space. They profit because improved public services and facilities, population growth, and the constructive efforts of surrounding property owners all boost the value of their properties.

Advisors Missed Getting at the Root

The D.C. mayor or Council periodically called on experts for advice on how to reduce revenue shortfalls and halt the outflow of residents and businesses.[6] A frequent recommendation was to call for more federal subsidies. The city does provide extensive services to the federal establishment and properly raises questions if reimbursement for these expenses is insufficient. But subsidies for its larger problems have not confronted the root causes of what ails the District.

Nevertheless, the League for Urban Land Conservation and the Pro-Housing Property Tax Coalition achieved some limited results. Their most evident impact was a growing awareness among officials and area citizens that an alternative way to raise public revenue was available. At public hearings about the Metro subway system, housing problems, and the future of the D.C. area, people unknown to the League or Coalition began "singing our song", so to speak. The Sierra Club, for example, urged the Maryland legislature to include the land tax in its Smart Growth measures to reduce sprawl in the D.C. area.

Property tax reform contains principles that should bring the left and right together. When the public has the wisdom and courage to confront the land issue and demand the reform to make Washington the world class capital it could be, politicians will be likely to listen. In the *Federalist Papers* (No. LI), "Publius" – a pen name attributed to Hamilton or Madison – wrote pointedly: "Justice is the end [point] of government. It is the end [point] of civil society. It ever has been and ever will be pursued until it be obtained, or until liberty be lost in the pursuit."

NOTES

1. Up to that time, officials were appointed by the White House. Members of the House and Senate District committees ruled the city, with more regard for how their oratory and enactments played back home, in Mississippi for example, than how their actions affected D.C. residents.
2. See Chapter 28 about the dramatic revitalization of Rosslyn in Arlington County to which Meyers referred.
3. Barry was intellectually keen and did much to elevate opportunities for his fellow blacks, but he later disgraced himself with drug use and other improprieties.
4. Orbis/Shepheard-Walwyn (Publishers), 1982.
5. Decades earlier, the District had adopted a "classified" system with separate and increasingly higher tax rates for the following categories of property: Class 1, owner-occupied homes; Class 2, multi-family residences; Class 3, hotel and commercial properties; and Class 4, all other uses. When vacant properties were singled out for a special rate, they constituted Class 5.
6. Among them were Andrew Brimmer, Alice Rivlin, and Philip Dearborn, all highly reputed economists with expertise in banking, budgets, and income taxation. Few who were on loan to the District during my half century in the area had credentials in land economics. Two exceptions were Dr Robert M. Schwab of Maryland University, who presented his research finding that a land tax did not have the negative effects of wage or sales taxes, and Dr Margaret Reuss of the University of the District of Columbia, who unsuccessfully urged a D.C. tax revision commission to endorse land value taxation.

19

In a Think Tank

THE URBAN INSTITUTE was hammered together under President Johnson shortly before his Administration was out and President Nixon's was in. Nixon's team started out, as is typical under most new presidents, confident that they knew what to do and how to do it. Then, again typically, reality set in. To help address welfare reform, health issues, and other items on their agenda, all "easier said than done", they looked for expertise and found much of it at the Institute.

Among Washington's think tanks trying to fashion policy solutions are the liberal-leaning Brookings Institution, the conservative-leaning American Enterprise Institute, and the libertarian Cato Institute. William Gorham formed the less ideological Urban Institute to provide technical guidance for new public programs and to evaluate existing ones. As editorial director, my challenge was to make the Institute's staff findings accessible to federal, state, and local officials.

Tax or Super-User Charge

Selma Mushkin, a highly regarded municipal finance specialist, directed an Institute project to examine user charges for services like urban transit, recreation, water, and waste handling. Not merely to raise revenue, user charges can be tailored to ration and conserve resources, reduce congestion, and enforce equity between users and nonusers.

In her book on this topic, *Public Prices for Public Products*,[1] Mushkin and public finance specialist Richard M. Bird discussed how to measure the benefits of a public improvement. They pointed out that "in some instances the most appropriate single measure of that benefit is property value". The taxation of increases in property value as a "reasonable proxy" for benefits from public services has "a long and venerable history", they noted.

Pondering this led me to conclude that a land tax is not a tax at all in the usual sense, but is more properly a super-user charge. "Super" seems to be the appropriate term because land values reflect the impact of *every* public service and facility that affects *every* site. "Super", because the land value of each parcel incorporates, in addition to these publicly-provided benefits, the impact of inherent natural features, the pressure of population density, and the totality of the surrounding built environment and enterprises. Land value sums up the worth of *all* the qualities the owner of a particular location has available to use and enjoy. Super, indeed.[2]

Simulations

The computer was just then coming into its own as a social science research tool. Urban Institute professionals pioneered in simulating America's welfare population and their model became much in demand to test the costs and effects of various welfare reform proposals coming down the pike. Computer programs were also developed to test transportation alternatives, inflation and employment relationships, and other economic puzzles that were previously beyond reach.

Institute staffers became intrigued with this new computer toy and the ability to search for causal relationships that would have been impossible or impractical with hand calculators. So much so, in fact, that when I asked some of them what useful guidance a city manager, for example, could glean from their work, they admitted they had gotten side-tracked. All was not lost. Learning how to devise social science simulations and regression analyses was useful in itself, so computer designers were encouraged to share their techniques with each other. That freed up the rest of the staff to devote full attention to practical solutions for public officials, from improved community policing to more equitable school funding to knowing when a public program should be extinguished.

A couple blocks from our offices, I stumbled into a very different world. I was getting a haircut from a Swedish barber and noticed that her walls were covered with the works of Jack Perlmutter, one of Washington's leading printmakers and a teacher at the Corcoran Gallery of Art. I asked about this array of treasures and the barber said her collection started years ago when Perlmutter was a struggling artist. He brought in a picture to pay for haircuts. After he used up his account, he brought another and another. In the heart of the nation's capital, where new technologies ran high finance and sophisticated research, I was fascinated that primitive economics, barter, was alive and well.

Spark of Interest

George Romney, President Nixon's Secretary of Housing and Urban Development, told Congress in 1970: "It is imperative to find ways to remove the present discouragement – and indeed to provide positive encouragement – for maintenance, repair, and rehabilitation of existing buildings and neighborhoods." That jolted me to do a think piece on how the upside-down tax system promotes blight.

Gorham, urbane, brilliant and well-connected, shared my piece with HUD's assistant secretary for research, who suggested we hold a symposium on the subject. Stars in the tax arena gathered for an all-day session exploring the economics of the property tax, assessment problems, political issues, research needs, and federal and state roles for improving the tax.[3]

The symposium let specialists share provocative ideas with each other. All favored correcting inequities in property tax administration, especially the under-assessment of land values. A large majority supported taxing land more and buildings less, yet the published report ignited no policy changes. Perhaps the rationale for the reform was not presented forcefully enough, or the time was not ripe.

Social change does not come easily. Of the hundreds of policy ideas floating around at a given period, what determines which ones move forward, which ones languish? The proposals that rise to the top are not necessarily the best ones but rather those that have champions who command the attention of citizens, politicians, and the media.

NOTES

1. Urban Institute, Washington, 1972.
2. See W. Rybeck, "The Property Tax as a Super User Charge", *The Property Tax and Local Finance*, C. Lowell Harriss, ed., Academy of Political Science, New York, 1983.
3. W. Rybeck, *Property Taxation, Housing and Urban Growth, a Symposium*, moderator, Urban Institute, Washington, 1970.

20

In the House

A REVOLTING DEVELOPMENT in California brought me to the inside world of Congress, not as a journalist any more but as a congressional staffer. Instead of confronting the daily puzzle – deciding which of Washington's circus rings were of most interest to readers – I had the privilege of working with others to see what could be done to improve the lot of the general public.

Good Tax Baby Thrown Out with Bad Tax Bathwater

California voters in 1978 approved Proposition 13, touching off an explosion of favorable national publicity. Howard Jarvis and his real estate clique promoted this "taxpayer revolt". Prop 13 capped property tax rates and froze assessments so they would revert to market value only when properties were re-sold.

Speaking about this to the International Association of Assessment Officials in Montreal, I predicted what any close observer of land policy could readily foresee, that California's land prices would go through the stratosphere. The revolt, I explained, was fueled by justified opposition to the injurious part of the property tax, the tax on improvements, but it dangerously whittled down the good part of the tax, the tax on land values.

My critique resonated with Representative Henry S. Reuss.[1] He had colorfully termed Prop 13 a "loose cannon careening around the deck of the ship of state". He asked me to be his assistant on urban issues. In that capacity my first project involved hearings and research leading to the report, "Proposition 13: Prelude to Fiscal

Distress or New Opportunities?"[2] Massachusetts and a dozen other states and localities adopted copycat measures in the wake of Prop 13. Our report was credited with contributing to subsequent voter turn-downs of similar proposals.

On grounds that voters overwhelmingly approved Prop 13, California's high court upheld the measure. Justices were not moved by the fact that businesses used tricky maneuvers to transfer properties without a "sale" to avoid triggering market-value reassessments. Worse, the justices were not disturbed that, under Prop 13, properties of identical values within the same jurisdictions were taxed differently, contrary to equal protection clauses in state and federal constitutions.

Bad things followed. Soaring land prices put housing out of reach for all but the affluent or for families daring to take on massive debt. With reduced property tax revenue, local governments cut back services and imposed stiff charges on services that formerly had been free. Prop 13 played no small part in the especially severe financial crisis that California experienced as the Great Recession struck the rest of the nation.[3]

Land Policy and Energy

The energy crisis of the 1970s motivated our next set of hearings, although the nation was not ready to deal seriously with this issue until another energy crisis flared up four decades later. Our report, "Compact Cities: Energy Saving Strategies for the Eighties",[4] presented incontrovertible evidence that urban sprawl is a gigantic waster of energy. Proponents of Smart Growth laws quoted this report. In enacting laws, however, states failed to incorporate key land tax policies for focusing growth within existing urban areas. Thus, despite Smart Growth's good sense and popular appeal, it has had minimal success in halting sprawl.

Billions of Metrodollars

Congressman Reuss wondered how Metro, the Washington area's not yet completed subway system, was affecting land values. Staffers Jerry Wade, Robert Josephs, Holly Stable, and Frank Getlein helped me design and carry out a research project that produced startling results. Metro, we found, had created new land value increases almost equal to the $2 billion-plus federal dollars expended on the project so far.[5]

From local realtors, assessors, developers, and appraisers we got data on sales and rents of sites near Metro stops and on comparable sites not served by Metro. Our ultra-conservative methodology only counted increased land prices around stations in operation, not increases already occurring around future stations. We calculated price impacts only two blocks from downtown Metro stops despite appraisers' evidence that locations twice that distance were experiencing price jumps.

A front-page *Washington Post* article quoted our conclusion that the biggest share of these billions of new land values were being pocketed by "people who were lucky enough to own land within easy access of Metro stations".[6]

Value capture, to let government recoup land values created by taxpayer funding of facilities like Metro, is now a topic discussed in transportation circles, but it has rarely been translated into action. The Washington, Virginia, and Maryland jurisdictions that fund Metro have shown little interest in recycling the values the facility generates. Instead, to meet the recurring budget shortfalls from federal, state, and local subsidies, Metro raises its fares. This reduces transit ridership, increasing the auto traffic and the resultant congestion and air pollution that Metro was designed to counteract.

If Land Data Were on the Sports Page

Inflation lowers real wages, destabilizes trade, and erodes confidence in the economy. Many signs point to land price escalation as a major factor in causing episodes of inflation. But where is the statistical evidence?

I posed this question to "Mr Federal Lands", as Marion Clawson was known. He was author of *Uncle Sam's Acres*, an authority on the Interior Department's Bureau of Land Management, and a leading expert on forestry, other natural resources, and urban fringe land markets. Clawson shook his head and answered, "Nobody's minding the store." He repeated it twice to make sure I heard his frustration. He called America's lack of full and reliable data about landownership and land prices appalling.

If only land were like football. Every detail about every team and every player is recorded. Readily available are data on wins, losses, scores, positions played, passes completed, yards run, touchdowns, injuries, receptions, interceptions, tackles, salaries, and sacks, with data per game, per season, and per career. Daily sports pages, sports magazines, and sports almanacs overflow with statistics. Baseball, basketball, tennis, golf, and other college and professional sports get this full court press by statistic keepers.

This is no tirade against games that bring joy or sorrow to fans, stir civic pride, and give us heroes to admire. Yet it says something about our national priorities that we provide voluminous information about spectator sports – everything one ever wanted to know and more – and that we gather a paucity of details about our economy's basic resource, our land. The limited statistics our governments collect tell us even less about our other national sport, land speculation.

Trying to "mind the store" and track the behavior and trends of local and national land markets became my last project with Reuss.[7] We determined that fully understanding and disclosing the ongoing land story necessitated formation of a national Land Price Index or LPI, comparable to the widely used CPI or Consumer Price Index.

Reuss in January 1979 released news of our plans to create an LPI. Secretaries of HUD, Labor, Treasury, Interior, and Commerce, as well as heads of the Federal Reserve Board and the Budget Bureau, applauded. So did Alfred E. Kahn, the White House inflation fighter, who was quoted in the *Wall Street Journal* as saying he saw "some value in old Henry's thesis".[8]

Top economists from federal agencies and the private sector eagerly joined our LPI task force. Grace Milgram, a respected housing and real estate analyst with the Congressional Research Service, chaired the effort. We had many work sessions and public forums. We studied whatever U.S. land data was available and collected and analyzed land data systems from other countries, some of which were quite good.

The Census of Governments every five years produced the most comprehensive report of U.S. real estate information: "Taxable Property Values and Assessment/Sales Price Ratios". John O. Behrens of that agency explained that data obtained from the states often lumped land and building values together or provided land values of dubious accuracy.

Economist Gene Wunderlich of the Agriculture Department noted a limitation of the farmland price data his agency collected.

Annual changes in the price of acreage used for growing wheat, for example, did not compare the same land from year to year. If a shopping mall replaced a wheat field, that land was omitted from the survey. Acres included in the wheat category one year might be in the corn category the next year. The National Association of Homebuilders' chief economist, Michael Sumichrast, indicated that similar problems of tracing the same properties plagued residential land data.

In short, statistics we looked at were incomplete, ambiguous, and incompatible with each other. To provide the big picture we came to see that the LPI needed to show the ups and downs of land prices nationally, by states, by metropolitan areas, by cities, and by major land use categories. It would need to show the value of raw natural resources, including those in federal lands leased to the private sector. And it should chart the degree of reliance on land taxes in all jurisdictions.

This project progressed to the point that the Bureau of Labor Statistics, with its long expertise in producing the CPI, took the tentative LPI design from our task force and began to estimate the start-up costs and also the annual costs of updating the index. Economists who kept track of our progress could barely wait to get their hands on the final product. They believed it would let them explore important issues that, in the absence of reliable statistics, they had been unable to properly address. Such issues included how much land values change due to population gains or losses; whether a city gets more "bang from the buck" by building a transit line or widening a highway; and whether land market data give advance warning signals of general economic distress.

Answers to such questions would be a long time coming.[9] When Ronald Reagan became President, his administration ordered the Bureau of Labor Statistics to halt its work on the LPI, effectively killing it. No reasons were given for this order, which would inhibit the federal government from understanding or dealing with land price inflation. This was no isolated instance. The Reagan administration terminated the Census of Governments' quintennial reports on property assessments. It closed down the Advisory Commission on Intergovernmental Relations which was engaged in strengthening state and local governments – something conservatives claim to be a high priority. It was a too-common example of the wide chasm between politicians' words and deeds.

Another Land Taxer

William J. Coyne's arrival in Washington coincided with the conclusion of my work with Reuss. I knew and admired Coyne as a Pittsburgh Councilman who led his city's expansion of the two-rate property tax. Coyne asked me to help him with press and urban policies in his new role as congressman.

For half a century Pittsburgh had taxed land at a rate twice as high as the rate on improvements. In 1978 the City Council was determined to avoid the fate of New York City, Cleveland, and other cities that were sliding into the red. Most Council members, therefore, were pushing for a hike in the wage tax.

Coyne asked Nobel economist Herb Simon of Carnegie-Mellon University to compare the impacts of wage and land taxes. Simon found that raising the same revenue from a higher land tax would cost average homeowners only $85 a year, while the wage tax would cost average workers $225 a year. The land tax won hands down. Pittsburgh kept its low tax rate on homes and other buildings and set the land tax rate four times higher than the rate on improvements.

Opponents predicted this would disrupt development and destabilize neighborhoods. The opposite happened. Building permits increased 32 percent over the previous year; vacant lot sales rose 17 percent, and new housing construction rose 15 percent. In the rest of Pittsburgh's metropolitan area, which used the conventional property tax, new housing declined 18 percent during the same period.

These results enabled Coyne to persuade Council to raise the tax rate on land again, to six times the rate on improvements. The further stimulus this gave Pittsburgh made him popular with voters, who elected him to Congress with big margins.

Because of Coyne's first-hand knowledge of local tax reform, I greatly enjoyed collaborating with him on speeches and op-ed pieces. Working with this kind, low-key, and conscientious public servant was a springboard for directing my attention to land issues in new ways and in a new venture.

NOTES

1. A Milwaukee Democrat, Reuss served in Congress from 1955 to 1982; chaired the House Banking, Finance and Urban Affairs Committee; inspired creation of Wisconsin's Ice Age Trail; earned a Bronze Star in World War II; and was deputy counselor of the Marshall Plan in Paris.
2. House Banking, Finance and Urban Affairs Committee, Subcommittee on the City, 1978.
3. Despite mounting evidence of Prop 13's negative impacts, it achieved sacred cow status. Voters, whose taxes are kept artificially low by the measure, have opposed its abolition to date. Prop 13 generated anti-tax and anti-government sentiments nationwide. Politicians, Ronald Reagan among them, and groups like the Tea Party movement have subsequently appealed to and magnified these sentiments.
4. Subcommittee on the City, House of Representatives, 1979.
5. "Metrorail Impacts on Washington Area Land Values", House Banking, Finance and Urban Affairs Committee, 1980.
6. "Land Around Metro Stations Increases $2 Billion in Value," *Washington Post*, January 24, 1981, p.1.
7. Some were surprised when Reuss retired. Early in his House career, Reuss observed aged members of Congress who lacked the stamina to perform. He proposed mandatory retirement at age 70. His measure failed but when Reuss reached that age he called it quits, even though the Washington press corps had just voted him one of the brightest members of Congress.
8. "Old Henry" referred not to Henry Reuss but to Henry George. Kahn and the *Journal* writer apparently surmised that land data would lead to wiser land tax policies, a la "Old Henry".
9. The Lincoln Institute of Land Policy in Cambridge, MA has been making strides in filling some of the statistical gaps relating to land policy.

21

Dialogue

IF AWARENESS OF the importance of land and resources to our nation's character is rare today, it was not always thus. In the early days of our Republic, John Jay, president of the Constitutional Convention and the first Chief Justice, expressed it this way:

> It has often given me pleasure to observe that independent America was not composed of detached and distant territories, but that one connected, fertile, wide-spreading country was the portion of our western sons of liberty. Providence has in a particular manner blessed it with a variety of soils and productions, and watered it with innumerable streams, for the delight and accommodation of its inhabitants.

I founded the Center for Public Dialogue to help cities and states struggling with fiscal difficulties, unemployment, housing problems, and declining downtowns become aware that attention to land policy would greatly ease these problems.

My approach was contrary to current mainstream thinking, but in sync with many great thinkers of the past. For example, William Blackstone, Britain's pre-eminent legal authority of the 1700s, whose commentaries on the law strongly influenced America's Founding Fathers, wrote: "The earth and all things therein are the general property of all mankind, from the immediate gift of the Creator." [1]

Previous work convinced me that systemic changes were needed. Pursuing such changes revealed the many hurdles that have to be overcome to chart a new course. Confronting those hurdles gave me unbounded respect for past reformers who persevered against great odds to advance social goals.

One curious hurdle is that many people want changed results without having to change their actions. "We've never done it that way" strikes them as a rational reason for rejecting proposed solutions.

Obviously, a major hurdle to changing existing arrangements – no matter how unfair or injurious those arrangements may be – is that certain people profit from those arrangements. They are prepared to fight furiously to maintain the status quo. Officials and citizens who lack the will or ability to buck these vested interests constitute a related hurdle.

Another hurdle is that cities, like people, can become addicted to relying on others to come to their aid. Federal and state subsidies enable localities to patch over their troubles. As long as it is possible for localities to continue wringing more grants and loans from higher levels of government, the pressure on them to search for ways to help themselves is relieved or postponed.

The greatest hurdle is the lack of understanding of the moral implications and practical consequences of current land policies. As Alexis de Tocqueville wrote in his perceptive analysis of the American experiment in democracy, "The nations of our time cannot prevent the conditions of men from becoming equal; but it depends upon themselves whether the principle of equality is to lead them to servitude or freedom, to knowledge or barbarism, to prosperity or to wretchedness."[2]

As its name implies, the Center's aim was to start overcoming these hurdles by injecting land issues into the public dialogue. Conferences and conventions of assessors, school superintendents, city managers, state legislators, economists, and county officials gave us platforms for our messages. We did research on pressing issues and disseminated our findings. We testified at public hearings. We provided analyses and recommendations for specific cities and states.

Housing vs. What It Sits On

The Center's report on affordable housing emphasized a fact that still has not penetrated the thinking of most officials dealing with this issue.[3] It is not the cost of *housing*, but the escalation of the costs of the *land under the housing*, that prices poor and moderate income families out of decent places to live. Calling a land crisis a "housing" crisis is not merely an inconsequential identification error; it draws attention away from the heart of the issue, leading policymakers to prescribe wrong and ineffective medicines.

Center reports for West Virginia and Washington State tried to focus attention on anticipated benefits from modernizing those states' land policies.[4] Our testimony before legislators of the District of Columbia, Maryland, Virginia, Missouri, California, New York, Minnesota, and other states was more pointedly targeted to critiques of pending laws and ordinances. We shared the good news that their governmental actions – providing public amenities of all kinds – were creating a treasure chest of land values, and that they could tap these values to ease many of their problems.

By giving away these publicly-created land values to well situated landlords, legislators leave themselves no alternative except to impose heavy taxes on labor and enterprise, hurting their economies and making themselves unpopular in the bargain.

A Tale of Five Cities

The documentary we produced to publicize progress being made with land taxes came about by chance more than design. The story begins with Agnes de Mille who, at age 78, had just made a heroic recovery from a stroke. Had she not become known as one of the foremost ballet and musical theater choreographers of her era, she surely would have gained fame for her passionate and eloquent writings and speeches attacking social injustice. Mrs Prude (Agnes's married name) asked Philip Finkelstein, director of the Henry George School in New York City, to explore the possibility of a TV series on themes relating to Henry George, her grandfather.

Finkelstein related this to me so I could ask the National Endowment for the Humanities in Washington if it were interested in supporting such a project. An Endowment historian told me she was fascinated by the rise of the Progressive movement of the late 1800s and that exploring George's role in it could be instructive. I agreed but stressed that Ms de Mille especially wanted to emphasize how George's ideas offered insights for resolving current problems. Betraying her youth, the historian replied, "Could anything that old really be pertinent today?"

As a matter of fact, I told her, Pennsylvania officials within a month were to meet at Valley Forge to hear how cities are benefitting by applying George's reform formulas. She responded with the wise advice to record that conference on film, which I arranged to do. The conference went well. Guerney Breckenfeld, a *Fortune* editor I invited, did his own research to verify what he heard at Valley Forge. His article about his findings, "Higher Taxes That Promote Development", appeared in his magazine's August 1983 edition.

Shortly after the conference, Finkelstein, in his fifties, died of a heart attack. Nobody replaced him to follow through on the TV series idea and I was left with reels of film. Unable to find anyone to take this gold mine of useful information, I decided in what must have been a lapse of sanity to make a documentary with it myself, although I had no inkling of what that entailed.

The film's asset was its useful testimony about the transformative powers of tax reform. But its format – a parade of talking heads – made it visually boring. So Erika and I visited the Pennsylvania cities discussed in the film, Pittsburgh, Harrisburg, Scranton, New Castle, and McKeesport. There we identified the most knowledgeable citizens and officials and returned with a film crew to record their experiences with the two-rate tax. A lot of cutting and splicing later, we came up with a draft.

We asked Father William Byron, then head of Catholic University, if one of his drama students might be our narrator. It turned out that Father Byron, during his earlier presidency of Scranton University, had been a friend and supporter of John Kelly, a Scranton land tax reformer who was in the film. Byron suggested that we ask William Graham, the head of his drama department, to be our narrator. Graham agreed and did a splendid job.

The premiere of *A Tale of Five Cities: Tax Revolt Pennsylvania-Style*, in a congressional hearing room, was crowded with press, "actors" in the documentary, and urban specialists. One speaker kindly predicted that the film would do for land policy reform what Rachel Carson's *Silent Spring* had done for the environment. Not by a long shot. Yet it received favorable news coverage and, over the years, was widely used by libraries, universities, housing activists, chambers of commerce, real estate boards, and tax reform groups.

Gradually the documentary became outdated for two reasons. First, Pittsburgh, the pioneer of the American land tax movement and the poster city of our documentary, abandoned the two-rate tax in 2000 after a badly botched reappraisal. The city's famous upward growth trend subsequently started to decline. The second reason, a good one, was that the story became a tale of ten, fifteen and more cities as other Pennsylvania jurisdictions got on the two-rate tax bandwagon.

The Center was gratified to be a part of that process as the telling of success stories helped engender further advances in Pennsylvania and elsewhere.

NOTES

1. *Commentaries on the Laws of England*, 1769, Vol. 1, Ch. 1, "Of Property in General".
2. *Democracy in America,* 1835, Book 1, Ch. 8.
3. "Affordable Housing – A Missing Link", W. Rybeck, Center for Public Dialogue, Kensington, MD, 1988.
4. "From Poverty to Prosperity by 2000: Prospects for Reviving West Virginia's Economy", Rybeck, CPD, 1992; "Look to the Land", Rybeck, Common Ground U.S.A., Seattle, WA, 1992.

PART V

FORGOTTEN CHAPTERS IN U.S. HISTORY

"IT TOOK THOUSANDS OF YEARS for our man-made laws to recognize the rights of the individual and to abolish slavery. Let us hope it will not take so long to recognize the rights of the community to collect what it produces." Thus John C. Lincoln concluded his short 72-page book, *Ground Rent, Not Taxes: The Natural Source of Revenue for the Government.*[1]

I had the privilege of knowing Lincoln, an inventor, industrialist and social reformer who stressed the moral imperative of collecting socially produced land values.

A broad-brush look at America's history sheds light on where our nation now stands and how we got here. The following accounts, with special attention to land issues, are intentionally selective, pointing to economic and social matters that tend to be omitted or glossed over. Uncovering these neglected aspects of our past has the felicitous outcome of pointing to ways that can help restore the health of our economic system.

NOTE

1. Exposition Press, New York, 1957.

22

America's Big Attraction

SCHOOLCHILDREN ARE TAUGHT that Europeans settled our country so they could freely practise their religions. This was certainly true for many colonists. Yet, according to letters and reports of those who came to America from the 1600s through the 1800s, an even greater lure induced multitudes to flee from places where their families had lived for generations, to cross the often treacherous Atlantic, to leave behind family members, and to give up familiar foods, customs, and cultures.

That big lure was *land*. Not just any land. Europe has abundant land. America's attraction was *free* or *cheap land*, lots and lots of it that was readily available to satisfy the immigrants' land hunger. To those who arrived on our shores, the contrast between Old World and New was striking.

In the Old World, farm hands typically received wages only sufficient to keep them strong enough to continue working for estate owners. No matter how long or skilfully they produced, they and their offspring looked forward, generation after generation, to remaining as servants to the lords of the lands on which they labored. Escape from their lowly status was rare.

In the New World, newcomers, including even indentured servants, were invigorated by the fact that the longer and smarter they worked, the more they prospered. Unlike their forebears, who had to pay steep rents for the "privilege" of working and eating, the immigrants kept the fruits of their labor. Settlers wrote with amazement about the abundant land that was within reach and rich beyond imagination – rich in great forests, fertile soils, fish and game, streams for navigation and water power – and, yes, rich in beauty to nourish the soul.

Pioneer life in America's early years was difficult, even perilous, almost unbearably so by modern standards, and romanticizing that life would be a serious distortion of history and a disrespect of the pioneers' hardships – except in comparison to what they and their families had left behind.

The Work Ethic

At the time of America's settlement, most people in the rest of the world toiled long and hard just to survive amid suffering and misery. Unfortunately, it takes no stretch of our imaginations to visualize those conditions. Those conditions still persist today in the world's areas of deep poverty.

The American work ethic became famous because it really paid to work. Americans took pride in standing on their own feet and in being able to see their families flourish. They took pride in all kinds of work. A current notion that some work is menial, beneath one's dignity, would have seemed bizarre to them. Without today's labor-saving devices, people had to work long at exceedingly arduous tasks. Yet every sort of work was glorified because it became obvious that those with good work habits and normal aptitude could advance themselves rather quickly. Nobody was siphoning off their earnings and savings. Society and individuals advanced together. As workers rose up the economic ladder, they enriched their communities as well.

Referring to this syndrome as the "Protestant work ethic" suggests that the work attitudes and practices were due to religious teachings. Perhaps so. But is it not likely that it was also the other way around? That is to say, the working atmosphere contributed to positive religious sentiments. Working on one's own land enabled people to reap what they sowed, without paying any overlord or royalty. Juxtaposed against Old World subservience and social immobility, the settlers' sense that they could control their own destinies led to a feeling that life was good, that all was right with the world. This fostered the can-do spirit and optimism that became dominant features of the American character. After centuries of stultifying feudalism, their liberating opportunities made it easier for early Americans to revere a Creator that enabled such a just social order to prevail.

Let the Liberty Bell Ring

Land not only spelled opportunity. It spelled liberty as well. *"Proclaim liberty throughout the land and to all the people thereof."* Our land-hungry forebears inscribed these words on America's famous icon, that cracked bell in Philadelphia. The settlers, well-versed in the Bible, knew that this inscription from Leviticus 25 was no mere praise for an abstract concept of liberty. They understood that it was a mandate *to free people smothered by debt and to preserve for everyone their birthright to a fair portion of land.*

"Proclaim liberty" was Moses' injunction to institute a Jubilee every fifty years to assure genuine liberty to a people that had endured an extended period of landlessness and slavery in Egypt. The call to proclaim liberty is followed in the Bible by specific instructions for how Israelites were to apportion the Promised Land once they reached it. Each tribe and each family within the tribe was to have its allotment of land.

Once that was done, why require another Jubilee every half century? Unlike philosophers who hypothesize Utopias populated with near-perfect humans, Moses anticipated that families could lose their lands due to poor harvests, personal misfortunes, mismanagement, stupidity, or wickedness. But he did not want human weakness or disasters to condemn future generations to a loss of their liberty. To forestall lands ending up in the hands of a few, as in the Egypt from which they had escaped, Moses devised a Jubilee land redistribution plan to restore equity and liberty to generation after generation. This land system as a basis for social justice proved effective for centuries.[1] The world would greatly profit from taking seriously Moses' prescriptions. No healing of economic ills is possible short of honoring his injunction to ensure that a powerful few do not take for themselves land rights that belong equally to all.

Is Jubilee outdated? The Mosaic mechanisms, yes. The concept of equal access to nature's earth, no. In a primitive agrarian society it was feasible to require people to pull up stakes and move their few belongings to different plots of farmland. To try to redistribute equal shares of land today, when people's factories, skyscrapers and homes – their private property – are firmly planted on the land, would involve severe injustices. Modern society requires new forms to achieve the goal of equalizing land rights. There are appropriate mechanisms applicable for modern society, as described in other chapters.

If ancient societies could discern how to form a just society, and how to deal with injustices that creep into societal processes, should not today's society with all the accumulated learning of the ages and all the modern investigative techniques know what needs to be done and how to do it?

The answer would be a resounding "Yes!" except for at least two factors. One is that old thinking and institutional arrangements have a momentum that is difficult in the extreme to reverse. A more potent factor is that those who enjoy wealth and control under outmoded arrangements work tirelessly to oppose change. It is a measure of their power to impede action that they have for so long succeeded in keeping necessary reforms out of the public spotlight.

We still need to hear the Liberty Bell ring.

NOTE

1. Some question whether the Jubilee system actually operated. John Kelly of Peoria, in his forthcoming book, *The Other Law of Moses*, offers convincing evidence that land restorations persisted for at least five hundred years and that, when prophets referred to liberty and justice, it was understood they were often talking specifically about Jubilee laws. Theologian Walter Brueggeman, discussing the Jubilee in *Land: The Foundation of Humanness*, wrote: "A crucial aspect of Jesus' mission was the reassertion of the land rights of the poor and displaced."

23

Old World Baggage

TOM PAINE WROTE: "Men did not make the earth. It is the value of the improvement only, and not the earth itself, that is individual property."[1]

When Paine was playing a leading role in generating popular support for American independence, his views about land were as ground-breaking as his opposition to the divine right of kings. Colonists at that time were enjoying opportunities that stemmed from access to America's natural bounties. This was *not* because they were taking Paine's advice to stop giving special privileges to landholders. They reaped these benefits *in spite of* inequitable feudalistic land practices that immigrants brought with them and then incorporated into rules of the colonies and the new republic.

Since European rules about landownership did not seriously impede America's dramatic growth, why even mention this Old World baggage? The contents of this baggage have gradually and stealthily crept back to endanger us. It is now critical to confront that particular baggage.

Many Rejected Institutions and Practices

We should be eternally grateful that our early leaders discarded a remarkable amount of baggage. They deserve boundless credit for the outmoded and unfair institutions they left behind, such as the following few examples.

Primogeniture was European law for some five hundred years. Under this law only the oldest sons could inherit a family's land.

Entail involved laws designed to prevent the breaking up of large estates, to keep them in the same family and to perpetuate a landed aristocracy.

Royal prerogatives included the deference and tribute owed to hereditary rulers.

Even though landowners predominated in the constitutional convention, they had the wisdom to avoid retaining those foundations of a rigid landowning class. Jefferson, John Adams, Madison, and Paine were instrumental in blocking "landed possessions" from becoming a qualification for voting or for election to Congress. Thanks to their unobstructed access to the earth's resources, our early pioneers and settlers became so self-sufficient and self-confident that the notion of bowing and scraping before kings, dukes, or other landed gentry struck them as ridiculous.

Earlier, when the first settlers arrived, natives shared their superb survival skills, enabling the pioneers to learn new ways of farming and hunting to stave off starvation. Europeans shared their more advanced material goods that often gave the Indians better lives. The initial examples of accommodation, with many Indians and settlers living peacefully near each other, and with land enough for all, suggests that the onset of an era of perpetual warfare was not as inevitable as the cowboy and Indian stories would have us believe. An opportunity to marry the two distinct cultures was missed to the detriment of both.

Land Rights, Land Wrongs

To whom did America's land belong? Since the time of Columbus, people rested their claims on the basis of various contradictory precepts – rights by virtue of authority, rights of discovery, rights by conquest, rights by rebellions, rights by purchase. (In all of these cases, "rights" should be understood as *assertion* of rights, without ascribing to them ethical justification.)

Rights by authority. No sooner was the New World discovered than Pope Alexander VI, in 1493, gave the entire New World to Spain.

A year later, still having little sense of the geography, the pope signed another papal bull, ceding what is now Brazil to Portugal. Conveniently ignored, of course, were the inhabitants with ancient roots in these territories.

British, French, and Dutch monarchs, also acting as if it never occurred to them that the Indians might have rights, granted North American lands to chartered merchant groups like the East India, Plymouth, and Hudson Bay Companies. Crowned heads carved out huge chunks of territory to favored individuals. William Penn was given Pennsylvania and Lord Ashley Cooper the Carolinas. King Charles II gave New Jersey to his brother James, who then sold absolute ownership to Sir George Carteret and John Lord Berkeley. Maryland was granted to Cecil Calvert, the first Lord Baltimore, who offered to any "adventurer" two thousand acres "for himself and his heirs forever" if he would bring five men to work the land and pay Lord Baltimore 400 pounds of "good wheat" annually.

Rights of discovery. Nations chose to ignore papal dictates and claimed territory wherever they were able to plant their flags. Finders keepers, in other words.

Rights by conquest. When flags and bulls were not respected, warfare ensued. Nations whose armies prevailed felt justified in holding on to the territories they won. Under this rule, one conquest did not preclude further conquests. Prized Caribbean islands, for example, changed hands multiple times. Might makes right.

Rights by rebellion. Our Declaration of Independence – plus winning the Revolutionary War – set the standard for this approach. People rose up, defying existing authorities, to say the land was theirs to control. America's rebellion inspired subjugated peoples elsewhere. European nations did not appreciate this standard when they lost colonies, and in the United States the North did not appreciate it when the South rebelled.

Rights by purchase. Those who claimed land by all these means often found it advantageous to exchange their holdings for a price. Grantees and trading companies often sold land in rather small parcels to attract people and, more than incidentally, to make the lands they retained more valuable. Massive property exchanges between nations included the 1803 Louisiana Purchase by the Jefferson administration from France, and the 1867 purchase of Alaska from Russia. Alaska was dubbed "Seward's Folly" until discovery there of gold, and later of oil, revealed what a bargain Secretary of State Seward had achieved.

TRINKETS AND TRICKERY

The standard tale is that Peter Minuit of the Dutch West Indies Company bought the island of Manhattan for a handful of beads worth only $24. Even if $24 was not a piddling amount in those days, they supposedly put one over on naïve Indians — in a friendly way, but highway robbery nevertheless.

Here's an alternative version of the event. Buying and selling land were alien concepts to the Algonquians. They were given rare beads, the likes of which they had never seen, for an island to which they never believed they held exclusive rights. Far from feeling robbed, the Algonquians found themselves akin to those legendary New Yorkers who, centuries later, coined the term "selling the Brooklyn Bridge" to describe selling something they didn't own to visiting country bumpkins.

Maybe the Dutch got the short end of the deal?

With hindsight it appears that Native Americans had a clearer sense of land rights than the immigrants who brought feudal values to their shores. Ironically, Indians became indoctrinated to the European model and now demand compensation for territories from which their ancestors were driven off, territories which their forebears never believed they owned in a monetary or exclusive sense.

Over time, right of purchase became the widely accepted norm and created a necessary and useful sense of order. It sanctified by law property deeds that, if traced back too far, would be questionable or worse. While the law provided a substantial degree of stability, the other side of the story is that, in practice, claims for the most treasured lands and resources were often obtained by trickery, scams, thievery, and other forms of lawlessness.

An especially bad part of the feudal baggage was the notion that individuals could properly amass as much land and resources as possible. Large landholdings became accepted as a fair measure of a person's or family's social worth. Those who monopolized strategically located lands found it easy to rationalize their control over fellow humans who needed access to "their lands" to survive.

Right of creation. Going not too far back, many American land claims are found to be based on force or fraud. Of course, if one goes all the way back, as title searchers would have us think they do, who is the original landowner of our America? Not even the Indians.

The underlying justification of *private* ownership is that property belongs to whoever creates it. By this measure, God or Nature is the rightful owner of the earth and its cornucopia of resources. As the Bible expresses it, "the Earth is the Lord's". From the times of the earliest settlers to this day, Americans have been inclined to keep this truth from influencing their behavior. The economic and environmental distortions stemming from not coming to grips with this truth have come home to roost, challenging us to change our ways.

NOTE

1. *Agrarian Justice*, 1797.

24

Land Grabbing, Land Abuse

THEOLOGIAN CHARLES AVILA WROTE: "The concentration of property in private hands began very early in Rome, based on legitimizing the absolute, exclusive individual ownership in land. Modern civilization has not yet discarded this antiquated ownership concept. This is one of the main roots of the present global crisis."[1]

In Europe, landholding was the pathway to power, wealth, and prestige. Being locked out of this pathway motivated many people to leave for America. Once here, however, many of them imitated their former overlords. Significant numbers tried to enrich themselves, not by work but by acquiring land, far more land than they could ever use.

The Dutch patroons in the Hudson River region got grants from the West India Company. Some of their manors embraced hundreds of thousands of acres.

Many Founding Fathers, George Washington among them, were avid land speculators. About three hundred miles from Mount Vernon, my adopted "Aunt" Henrietta lived on Washington Farms, so called because our first president as a young man claimed this huge tract on the hills above the Ohio River near Wheeling. He later gave this holding to his half-brother Lawrence.

Land monopolization and absentee ownership took root early in the colonial era, leaving no room for thinking about ways to share the land equally with the Indians. The land-grabbing frenzy and the rapid expansion of the newcomer population were major factors

134

in driving natives off territories they had occupied for centuries, sparking a long, sad period of warfare.

Plantation owners, meanwhile, were hard pressed to meet foreign and domestic demand for cotton, tobacco, and other crops. To turn out more produce than they could generate by themselves and their local farm hands, they imported slaves. Future generations will find it harder and harder to believe how long it took before it became abundantly evident that slavery violated the most basic ideals and ethical guidelines that our nation proudly proclaimed.

A bloody and wrenching Civil War was sparked less by human rights issues than by North-South differences over state rights, tariffs, and economic issues. In the end, however, it did result in banishing slavery. America still has not fully recovered from the consequences of that inhumane institution. Challenges to erase racial animosities and inequities remain, notwithstanding the milestone election of a black President in 2008.

Alexander Hamilton led the push for government expansion of public works, especially canals for barge traffic and turnpikes for stagecoaches, horses and wagons to connect remote areas and spark trade. Steam-powered factories, boats, and trains were among the inventions that transformed manufacturing and transportation. The placid farm-based society of the pre-Revolutionary period soon gave way to a flurry of industrial activity. This was marked with ups and downs.

Those who were surprised by the 2008 economic meltdown were not paying attention to America's history of repetitive business cycles. Journalist-economist Fred Harrison of Britain[2] and investment advisor Phillip J. Anderson of Australia[3] have both carefully documented the U.S. economy's periodic troughs and peaks that occurred with uncanny regularity.

Growing commerce and industry gave the country innumerable constructive results. But corruption, destruction and waste marked their exploitation of natural resources. Timber barons had their lumbermen clear-cut magnificent forests farther than the eye could see. Agents of the coal barons tricked Appalachian homesteaders into practically giving away titles to the coal under their properties, and with fine print that gave the residents no legal recourse if the mines polluted their wells or caused surface acres to collapse. Large corporate combines cornered the rights to minerals, oil, and gas, stifling competition.

Land was a major factor in the rise and demise of the great railroads. The government gave away vast amounts of the public domain to railroad companies to spur their westward expansion. Many railroad empires then milked and neglected their rail operations while they concentrated on real estate deals.

Laws were stretched to condone or overlook the reckless plunder of our resources, not surprising in light of the exploiters' practice of padding the pockets of high officials. Public outcry to curb these abuses increased after the Teapot Dome scandal revealed bribery and corruption in the federal leasing of rights to exploit vast oil reserves. The Sherman Antitrust Act and other measures were enacted with the aim of preventing unbridled desecration of our natural bounty by monopolists.

Despite reform attempts, the continuing destructive maneuvers by huge business conglomerates looked like a sure-fire formula for undoing America's remarkable growth. The next chapter explores why America, in the face of these hurtful practices, continued to grow and prosper.

Notes

1. *Ownership: Early Christian Teachings*, Orbis Books, Maryknoll, NY, 1983.
2. *The Power in the Land* , Shepheard-Walwyn, London, 1983.
3. *The Secret Life of Real Estate*, Shepheard-Walwyn, London, 2008.

25

Three
Saving Graces

GIVEN THE CHAOTIC RECORD of land claims based on force and chicanery, given the successful efforts of numerous colonists to become landed gentry in the Old World manner, and given the reckless abuse of natural resources, how did the newly independent America manage to forge a new burst of freedom and prosperity that amazed and inspired the rest of the world? Three factors combined to stave off disaster – land taxation, the frontier, and a market that was still basically highly competitive.

One – A Marvelous Source of Public Revenue

Revolutionary Americans hated despots but they were not opposed to government. Their new civilization required a full deck of public amenities, and the sooner the better. They needed a justice system with sheriffs, judges, courts, and jails to control unscrupulous and rowdy elements; schoolhouses and teachers for the children; public water supplies for health and sanitation; dams for water power to keep the mills running; and ports, canals, and roads to facilitate commerce and to keep people connected throughout their largely rural and small-town nation.

How would the infant republic finance local governments to carry out these tasks?

Note the emphasis on *local* government. Unlike today, the federal government initially took responsibility for far fewer functions and it met its unbelievably low budgets largely from customs duties. Citizens had become accustomed in the colonial era to local rule. People they knew ran the state assemblies. In their town meetings, ordinary citizens like themselves ran the show at the community level. After independence, Americans almost automatically continued to look to their cities, counties, and states for meeting most of their public needs.

Revolutionary Americans wanted effective self-government. The property tax was their chosen instrument to provide public revenue. This was a monumentally important choice.

The constant drumbeat of attacks on the property tax over the past half century precondition people to have a knee-jerk reaction against believing anything good about this tax. Those who condemn the tax are half right. Taxing homes and other buildings discourages their construction and maintenance, far from desirable goals. But they are also half wrong – exceedingly wrong – not to praise and support the taxing of socially created land values.

The colonial and post-Revolutionary property tax was not a pure land tax. Nevertheless, considering that the bulk of improvements in those days tended to be humble shops, dwellings and farm buildings, the revenue came overwhelmingly from the location value of the land itself.[1] Land owners accepted their duty to pay for the privilege their holdings conveyed, so the tax did not appear to be unpopular. It had many virtues that deserve to be underscored:

- The land tax served as an *opportunity equalizer*. Those with the most productive and desirable sites paid more, those with poorer parcels paid less.
- The tax *favored small holdings*. The fiscal burden imposed on people "stuck" with large holdings restrained the concentration of landownership to a considerable degree.
- The tax was not sufficiently steep to halt all land grabbing, but it prodded estate holders to sell off excess unused lands and thus *prevented land scarcity*. "Scarcity" of land is an odd term because the quantity does not change. But when owners refuse to sell to those who need it, the land available for use appears scarce. A tax that results in bringing land on the market adds to the *effective* supply.
- The land tax *rendered land speculation less profitable* by discouraging land hoarding.

Land taxation set the stage for economic progress. Few accounts of America's stunning economic growth give adequate credit to the way the land tax contributed to this phenomenon. Its role may be clarified by comparing development in South America and the United States.

Latin American colonization had a big head start of about a century. Conquistadores took dominion over vast territories of Central and South America in the 1500s. Portuguese and Spanish colonists converted natives into a servant class and put them to work building cathedrals, forts, and attractive towns. How could the infant United States of the 1700s and early 1800s with its crude buildings, primitive towns, and scattered homesteads catch up to, let alone surpass, these impressive colonies to their south? In today's terminology, the United States was Third World compared to "developed" and "advanced" Latin nations.

South America's landholding class had virtually no land taxes for several centuries. With no restraint against land monopoly, their countries became locked into feudal systems. Small oligarchies at the top grew exceedingly affluent, rarely by being enterprising but usually by exacting rents and forced labor from the large and very poor class at the bottom of the scale.

This arrangement caused economic stagnation at the time the United States economy began to gather steam. The hard-working Latino underclass, without their own farms or workshop sites, could not begin to match the ingenuity and vitality of the people to the north whose access to land gave them a liberating sense of mobility and let them become their own masters. Land taxation made a difference.

From the 1700s until the early 1900s, the property tax was virtually the sole support of U.S. state and local governments. To this day it remains the single most important revenue source for most cities, despite politicians who make the property tax their favorite whipping boy. The hundreds of billions worth of real estate taxes fund about 75 percent of local budgets. Taxes on improvements yield an estimated 60 percent of the annual property tax revenues; taxes on land yield around 40 percent of the total.[2]

Two – Beyond the Horizon

The U.S. frontier meant many things. Hardy men, women, and children heading West in Conestoga wagons. Gold rushes. Vast prairies. Rugged Rocky Mountains. Romantic explorers. Cowboys and Indians. In economic terms, however, the frontier was America's *magnificent safety valve.* As famously described by historian Frederick Jackson Turner, the frontier moderated the impact of inequities and incongruities in our early land and economic policies.

When cheap land became harder to find along the Atlantic Seaboard, or when factory owners and shopkeepers paid too little to satisfy workers, people did not have to suffer. They could "go West, young man," as Horace Greeley advised. Most people stayed put, but those employees who did take flight caught the bosses' attention, inducing them to boost wages to hold those who remained behind.[3]

If folks in the East yearned for adventure or a chance to start life afresh, they could head off to that expanse of open land. The knowledge of the frontier's escape hatch, whether used or not, became part of the American psyche and advanced better living conditions throughout the nation.

With access to land, labor was king. This does not imply that labor lived in the lap of luxury. Far from it. Life on the frontier was difficult, not idyllic. Wages on farms or in shops and factories should not be idealized as munificent either. Workers were kings in the sense that they could be independent, not easily led by others.[4] Available land became the *sine qua non*, the essential ingredient, of an equitable thriving society for everyone. For "everyone," sad to say, provided you were of European stock and were not Indian, Black, Chinese, or otherwise an "outsider".

The Homestead Acts, begun under President Abraham Lincoln during the Civil War, enabled those headed west to gain a foothold on the earth. Living and working on 160 acres for five years gave them title to that part of the vast public domain. Reflecting the then common sentiment that land monopolization obstructs job opportunities, Lincoln said, "The land, the earth God gave to man for his home, sustenance and support, should never be the possession of any man, corporation or society, any more than the air or water – if as much."

Three – "Fair" Capitalism

The blacksmith, printer, trapper, orchard grower, toolmaker, clothing shop owner, and all other producers kept for themselves what they earned in wages and profits. For a century most Americans paid no taxes on incomes, sales, gross profits, or investment earnings.[5]

Adam Smith published *The Wealth of Nations* in 1776, the year of the Declaration of Independence. America's infant democracy and the free market capitalism postulated in Smith's book were siblings growing up together. America put into practice the Scottish economist's theory of minimal governmental interference with production, opportunity for all, special privileges for none, and open competition. These elements were once hallmarks of liberalism. However, liberals and conservatives have switched positions so frequently that these labels tend to lose their meaning.

Smith's *laissez faire* concept of a largely unfettered economic system was in sharp contrast to the prevailing mercantilist policies under which European nations controlled production, trade, and labor. However, those who characterize Smith as favoring "anything goes" offer an inaccurate caricature of his proposals. Government, according to Smith, must set frameworks and limits. To use a baseball analogy, equitable rules and umpires to enforce them come first. After the umpire says, "Play ball," he does not help or obstruct the athletes, provided they comply with the rules.

The father of capitalism was prescient about the threats to a free market. He criticized monopolies and other obstructions to genuine competition. He warned against oppression of laborers and farmers by business combines and powerful ecclesiasts and aristocrats.

Smith was particularly outspoken on the efficacy of taxing land values, which he referred to as "ground-rent" or "ordinary rent". The following quotations from *The Wealth of Nations* may instruct and perhaps astound mainstream economists who, for several decades, have wrangled over how to improve our tax system without considering, or even mentioning, land tax alternatives:

> Ground-rents are a still more proper subject of taxation than the rent of houses. A tax upon ground rents would not raise the rents

of houses. It would fall altogether upon the owner of the ground-rent, who acts always as a monopolist, and exacts the greatest rent which can be got for the use of his ground...

Both ground-rents and the ordinary rent of land are a species of revenue which the owner, in many cases, enjoys without any care or attention of his own. Though a part of this revenue should be taken from him in order to defray the expenses of the state, no discouragement will thereby be given to any sort of industry. The annual produce of the land and labour of the society, the real wealth and revenue of the great body of people, might be the same after such a tax as before. *Ground-rents, and the ordinary rent of land, are, therefore, perhaps the species of revenue which can best bear to have a peculiar tax imposed upon them* [emphasis added]... Nothing can be more reasonable than that a fund which owes its existence to the good government of the state, should be taxed peculiarly, or should contribute something more than the greater part of other funds, towards the support of that government.[6]

Unlike other taxes, a tax on land values reduces its selling price because, as Smith observes, "The more the inhabitant was obliged to pay for the tax, the less he would incline to pay for the ground." He thus affirmed why America's heavy taxation of land values throughout the 1800s was effective in keeping access to land affordable.

Happy Confluence

Grassroots democracy thrived in this fortunate mix of land taxes, an open frontier, and free markets. Close-to-home governments kept order and provided essential services and facilities. Equality of opportunity was in large measure a consequence of the widespread availability of nature's gifts. Most people found free or cheap sites for their homes and work places and easy access to the resources needed for growing and manufacturing things. Vigorous competition promoted inventiveness and efficiency in the making, selling, and distribution of goods. Neither governments nor landlords were claiming big shares of the fruits of other people's labors.

The picture just painted reveals significant themes that predominated America's pioneering experiments in democracy. This was the America that people around the globe saw as a beacon of hope. Lurking in the underbrush, however, was the exploitation of resources that was to become more threatening as time went on.

Analysis of the elements responsible for our nation's early vitality points to the kinds of policies needed to replicate those elements to meet today's challenges.

NOTES

1. John Adams, Jefferson, and Paine proposed heftier taxes on large landholdings. Paine argued strenuously for taxing land values *only* and for removing taxes on improvements.
2. For a comprehensive analysis of the role of the U.S. property tax, including historical statistics, see W. Rybeck, "United States" chapter in *Land Value Taxation Around the World*, 3rd edition, R.V. Andelson, ed., Blackwell Publishers, Malden, MA, 2000.
3. Adam Smith observed in 1776 that North American wages were considerably higher than in technically advanced Britain where "the landlord demands a share of almost all the produce which the labourer can either raise or collect". *The Wealth of Nations*, Random House, New York, 1937, p.65.
4. It seems likely that one reason European workers were quicker to unionize and plea for welfare measures was their lack of a frontier and access to land, which would have empowered them.
5. Some states did expand what they called the "general property tax" to try to tax accumulated wealth. The federal budget remained relatively picayune until it expanded to finance the Civil War.
6. Adam Smith, *The Wealth of Nations*, Random House edition, 1937, pp.795-6.

26

Fundamentals
Forgotten

WHAT MADE AMERICA DEPART from elements that produced a level of prosperity the world had never seen? The country had enjoyed a rare degree of upward mobility that freed citizenry from a constricting sense of class. Boldly independent, people nevertheless united in pride of their country and its democratic institutions.

Key elements behind this success, to recapitulate, included reliance on land taxes, a competitive market system, and a near absence of taxes on labor and capital. These ingredients have so faded from the public dialogue that the bulk of economists and policymakers appear to suffer from a case of mass amnesia.

Feudal land policies, as noted, initially were neutralized by an abundance of richly endowed lands that served as a banquet table for the sparse population of the early republic. But the Old World baggage caught up with us. Pursuit of wealth, not from enterprise but from landholding, proved damaging as floods of new immigrants came to enjoy America's "streets paved with gold". Of course, immigrants who took this literally were shocked to find streets like rivers of mud when wet and full of choking dust when dry. Their living quarters and public amenities often were inferior to those they had left behind. Yet such disappointments tended to be forgotten as they breathed the fresh air of freedom.

All Fenced In

What about our frontier, the potent economic escape hatch that held unemployment in check and acted as a countercheck to the tendency to set wages excessively low? By around 1900 the most desirable and productive public lands were either doled out or retained in permanent federal preserves. The vanishing frontier marked a substantial weakening of the economy's resilience and a weakening of labor's bargaining power.

Land-grabbers became absentee owners after fraudulently amassing large quantities of public domain lands that were originally dispensed under the Homestead Act of 1862, the Timber Culture Act of 1873, and the Desert Land Act of 1877. Congress designed all of these acts to benefit genuine small farmers of the type visualized by Jefferson and Lincoln.

Rape of the Land

In the mid and late 1800s, corporations denuded whole counties and states of their primeval forests. They used shady methods to acquire rights to coal, oil, natural gas, iron, and other minerals.

Looking back, if states had put fair market values on these resources and taxed them accordingly, such practices might have been averted and America could have husbanded its natural gifts in a manner environmentalists now endorse. That did not happen for at least three reasons:

First, the interests that were ruthlessly depleting resources helped elect and finance key governors and legislators. Plunder of resources went unchecked, as did the exploitation of lumberjacks, drillers, rail builders, and miners, who did the dirty work.

Second, people had become so used to the abundance of resources that they overlooked the excesses of the land-grabbers and tended to admire them for their resourcefulness, to use a bad pun. The differences between common property and private property, and the different responsibilities they entail, were absent from the vocabulary.

Third, human nature led many to hope that someday they too could become land-grabbers. Others were not sufficiently aroused to push for regulating or prosecuting those who were raping the land.

Land Booms, Land Busts

Land speculation did not prosper until rapid population growth occurred across America. As demand for choice sites heated up, land speculators could buy locations in the path of growth and exact tolls from people needing those sites. This pushed up land prices to the point where production was stymied, touching off one of the country's first major economic crises, the Panic of 1837.

Recovery began when land prices subsided. Further panics, depressions, or recessions occurred about once every generation. Land booms begat land busts. The Great Depression left indelible memories, but Americans have exhibited a strange loss of memory about the frequency of these recurring crises. Each bust wipes out the savings and jobs of innocent victims who were not involved in speculative activities. Each bust chips away at public confidence in the market system, leading people who are suffering to call for – or more often to demand – government intervention and aid.

When Illinois Senator Paul H. Douglas headed the National Commission on Urban Problems, he addressed the land speculation scenario:

> The owners of the land can go to Hawaii and rest languidly on the beaches or make prolonged safaris into the innermost regions of Africa. They may study Shakespearian literature at Stratford on Avon, or Zen Buddhism in Japan, or ponder urban problems in Washington. They can go up in space capsules or down a hole in the ground. They will become richer and richer without toil or sweat.

Bigger and Bigger

With the technical advances of the Industrial Revolution, the manufacturing sector outpaced agriculture, changing the nation from a rural to an urban society. Americans still romanticize family farms and mom-and-pop businesses, but these were relegated to the minor leagues as corporate farms and gigantic corporations rose to dominance by gobbling up small enterprises. Corporations often confronted rivals, not by trying to out-compete them but by buying them up. They monopolized the finished products and acquired

PERILS OF A 'GOOD' DEPRESSION

When government and the people are borrowing too heavily and spending recklessly, some are heard to say that we need a "good depression" to knock sense into our officials and citizens.

When old Uncle Stanley is eating all the wrong things and not exercising, does his family say he needs a good heart attack? It might make him change his ways, but then again it might prove fatal.

Economic heart attacks are perilous too. Citizens who suffer losses are demoralized, especially when those who helped cause the crash emerge unscathed or even richer. Demagogues and hate-mongers have a field day. Desperate people cry out for food and shelter. Responding to pleas for help at any cost, officials put prudence, traditional safeguards, and civil liberties on hold as they try to provide relief. Some who escape the suffering heartlessly object to rescue efforts and argue that massive failure – a good depression? – is a necessary corrective. A safer and saner route is to resurrect the "secret" formula from earlier days to restore the conditions that put America on the road to prosperity.

the raw resources and the entire chain of production, literally from the ground up.

"Trust busting" began in earnest under President Teddy Roosevelt and during the early 1900s, the heyday of investigative reporters known as muckrakers. Congress during the Great Depression created new laws and new federal agencies to try to further constrain giant combines and prevent obstructions to competition.

Yet the march of monopoly has not slowed. Almost no attention has been given to the anti-competitive aspects of land and resource acquisition on a large scale. Resulting high land prices sap the vitality of small businesses and block the entry of new ventures.

Speculators who "farm" land values in rural areas force out real farmers.

A curiosity is that the business and manufacturing lobbies that rail against the inefficiencies, waste, and cross purposes of large government bureaucracies never seem to recognize or admit that large businesses are prone to these same defects.

Shift from Local to Federal Power

The Civil War preserved the Union and ended slavery, but its high financial costs became a rationale for instituting the income tax.

Those who decry the steady shift of power from localities and states to Washington tend to ascribe this to an ideological or socialistic conspiracy. The fact is that mobilizing for wars moved us in this direction. The Great Depression pushed us further. When local governments were incapable of helping families meet their most basic needs, the federal government stepped up to the plate. It did so, not conspiratorially, but to rescue the hungry and the jobless, and to stave off riots or rebellion, fear of which was not unrealistic when everything was collapsing for millions.

Why were local governments not up to the task? One major reason was the transformation of the property tax. It had evolved to become primarily a tax on residential, commercial, and industrial structures as opposed to its earlier role as a force to recoup community-created land values. Although the constructive part of the property tax, on land values, persists and gives America a leg up on nations that do not tax land at all, the good it does is greatly diminished by the destructive effects of the tax on improvements. This made the tax increasingly unpopular and put a ceiling on how much revenue local officials could derive from it.

Instead of modernizing their property tax, states and cities turned to new taxes on wages, profits, sales, and anything else they could think of. Many of these, along with relatively low taxes on land values, contributed to the decline of cities. This in turn led local governments to join the clamor for help from Washington. To repeat, the federal government kept growing in response to pleas from the home front, not, as the John Birch Society, many Tea Party voices and strident talk show commentators insist, from a sinister ideological conspiracy.

After out-of-control land prices helped plunge the nation and countries around the world into economic disaster, one would have expected to see a spotlight on land policy. One would also expect this issue to come to the front burner when the natural resources we use – and how we use them – are involved in the global warming crisis. Despite the convergence of these land issues, our federal and local governments lack a policy framework for getting on top of these problems.

This is where the pragmatic and ethical ideas of Henry George re-enter the picture.

27

Competing
Philosophies

"I PROPOSE," WROTE HENRY GEORGE, "to seek the law which associates poverty with progress, and increases want with advancing wealth; and I believe that in the explanation of this paradox we shall find the explanation of those recurring seasons of industrial and commercial paralysis which, viewed independently of their relations to more general phenomena, seem so inexplicable."

Keen observer, painstaking analyst, brilliant intellect, powerful writer and orator, original economist, moralist to the core, this was George. His fascinating life was quintessentially American.[1] In his day, his call for justice with an essentially pro-enterprise slant created an international sensation, but it was soon overshadowed by the anti-capitalist thesis of Karl Marx and, later, by the government-directed correctives urged by John Maynard Keynes and others.

George undoubtedly will in good time be appreciated as one of America's finest. If the enterprise system is again to become free and vibrant, enabling democracy to live up to its high ideals, it will happen in no small part because George's philosophy and prescriptions will be put into play.

Ahead of His Time

In 1879, when George's *Progress and Poverty* thrilled workers with its vision of social equity, American critics could still ask seriously, "What land problem?" Viable expanses of the frontier still existed. Cities were not yet sprawled over the countryside. Farmland and forests seemed to go on forever. And reasonable people could expect that the natural resources feeding our burgeoning industrial machine were ushering in a new era of well-being for all. An era of prosperity did follow but a rising standard of living camouflaged the fact that prosperity was not "for all".

The subtitle of George's book, "An Inquiry into the Causes of Industrial Depressions and of Increase of Want with Increase of Wealth ... the Remedy", also raised questions. Despite periodic panics, the post-Civil-War citizenry did not agree that the capitalist system was in trouble. Andrew Carnegie, the Scottish native who rose to become America's top steel magnate-monopolist and then philanthropist, propounded the comforting belief that civilization was on a permanent upward climb.

The optimism ingrained in our national character supported this faith in Progress with a capital "P". None could deny the low wages, unemployment, and misery that George portrayed. However, so many American families had extricated themselves from poverty that they were more likely to blame the poor than imperfections in the economic order.

Vested Interests

While the mass of Americans had no awareness of the connection between land policies and the economic opportunities available to them, the importance of land was neither forgotten nor ignored by the upper-upper class.

Unlike many speculators who bought land to sell later at a profit, John Jacob Astor acquired Manhattan parcels to hold on to in order that, as specified in his will, his family could forever garner the increasing rental values from leaseholders. William Ogden, Chicago's first mayor, worked to make his city a rail center to bolster the value of his own real estate holdings. How well he succeeded is revealed in his diary, which noted that a property he bought in 1845 for $15,000 grew in value to $10 million by 1865; and that another he purchased in 1844 for $8,000 sold eight years later for $3 million.[2]

Nobody can credibly suppose that the riches from landholding were not uppermost in the minds of coal barons who sent agents out to Appalachia to buy coal rights out from under poor homesteaders at roughly a dollar an acre.

By the end of the 1800s, a single company, the United States Steel Corporation, had acquired ownership or control through leases of most of the iron ore ranges of the Great Lakes area.

The point is that wealthy families and corporations were enriching themselves by monopolizing enormous quantities of prime urban sites, fertile farmland, forests, natural gas, oil, and other raw materials. Imagine their reaction when Henry George insisted that the gifts of nature belonged not to a select few but to society in general. When his book became a worldwide bestseller and land taxers grew to such an extent that political action seemed imminent, landed interests fought back.

These vested interests succeeded in getting many states to specifically prohibit land value taxation. Ironically, while posing as protectors of private property, they supported shifting taxes on to genuine private property – homes, office buildings, industrial plants, wages, and the rest – in order to retain their ability to siphon off the common property of society.

Prominent economists whose theories George punctured also fought back defensively. Men with large fortunes, delighted to find opponents of George in academic circles, made sure these anti-Georgists gained prominent seats in the economics departments of the universities they endowed. A plethora of books, articles, speeches, and courses denouncing George gradually succeeded in painting him as an idealistic crank whose ideas were unworkable and dangerous.[3]

To circumvent the logic of George's analysis and proposals, his academic opponents chose a bizarre path. *They took land out of their theories of economics!* Classical economists, whatever their many differences, recognized as self-evident that the basic factors in the creation of wealth are land, labor, and capital. George built on this solid classical foundation, adding new insights.

When neoclassical theorists decreed that land as a distinct factor no longer existed, they redefined land as a category of capital. It recalls Lincoln's quip: "If you call a tail a leg, how many legs does a dog have?" Land is no more capital than a tail is a leg. This false definition left economic toolkits devoid of essential land policy instruments. Policymakers slid down slippery slopes as they denied the following clear distinctions between land and capital:

• Humans create capital. Humans do not and cannot create land.

- Capital is wealth, used to create more wealth. Land cannot be used to create more land, but it is the source from which labor and capital create wealth.
- The supply of capital can vary. The supply of land is essentially fixed. As Will Rogers famously advised, "Buy land, they ain't making any more."
- Increased demand for capital tends to lead to more capital, often at lower prices, assuming open competition. Increased demand for land leads to no additional land but simply raises the rental value or price of land.
- Taxing capital raises its selling price. Taxing land reduces its selling price.

The collapse of totalitarian communism in the Soviet Union and the failings of many other communist regimes may make it difficult now for younger generations to understand Marxism's appeal and its initial ability to nearly eclipse the Georgist movement.

Karl Marx, like George, was appalled by the social ills of his times, and many of his criticisms rang true. Their approaches for treating the failings could not have been more divergent. Marx wanted to tear down and replace the entire capitalist structure. George wanted to repair the structure and make it work equitably. Marx favored revolution, George evolution.

From a salesmanship perspective, moreover, Marxism had a clear advantage. It gave exploited and angry people a villain – the capitalists – to blame for all their problems. In contrast, long before cartoonist Walt Kelly had Pogo say in a comic strip, "We have met the enemy and he is us," George concluded that the people themselves had to change their own thinking and use democratic machinery to correct social ills, a position that did not lend itself to demagoguery.

Marxism attracted single-minded zealots willing to conspire through secret cells, follow orders from above, adhere to a strict party line, and overlook evil behavior by their leaders in the belief that the ends justified the means. Georgism attracted individualists who pursued their own varied strategies, eschewed party discipline, and put their faith in education, the free market of ideas and democratic processes.

Under the Radar

While communist regimes were racking up failures, the validity and potency of the Georgist approach was being demonstrated where its style of reforms had been adopted. These examples of constructive land tax applications have attracted surprisingly little publicity outside the land economics community. The next section therefore spotlights a number of these success stories.

_____

NOTES

1. Biographies include: Charles A. Barker, *Henry George*, Oxford University Press, New York, 1955; Henry George, Jr., *Life of Henry George*, Doubleday & McClure, New York, 1900 (republished by Chelsea House, New York and London, 1981); George Geiger, *The Philosophy of Henry George*, McMillan, New York, 1933; Steven B. Cord, *Henry George: Dreamer or Realist*, University of Pennsylvania Press, Philadelphia, 1965. For a typical distortion and belittling of George's views, see the chapter about him in Gerald W. Johnson, *Lunatic Fringe*, Lippincott, Philadelphia, 1957. For a thorough discussion of arguments opposing George's views, see Robert V. Andelson, ed., *Critics of Henry George*, Associated University Presses, Cranbury, NJ, 1979. For more complimentary views, see Will and Dorothy Burnham Lissner, eds, *George and the Scholars*, Robert Schalkenbach, New York, 1991.
2. Quoted in Aaron M. Sakolski, *Land Tenure and Land Taxation in America*, Schalkenbach, New York, 1957.
3. For accounts of attacks on George by professional economists and their wealthy backers, see Mason Gaffney and Fred Harrison, *The Corruption of Economics*, Shepheard-Walwyn, London, 1994.

PART VI

LIVING
LABORATORIES

THE POLICY CHANGES proposed in these pages are not abstract theories. They reflect concrete applications. Publicly-created land values are being collected in varying degrees in a range of localities. Each instance constitutes a kind of living laboratory that provides an opportunity to observe the impact of land value taxation.

The good news is that injurious tax systems that weaken the enterprise system, reduce real wages, and generate distrust of government can be overcome. Successful reforms in jurisdictions that have led the way paint an optimistic picture of what the future can hold. Healthier cities, ample job opportunities, more affordable housing, and reduced sprawl are attainable. As philosopher-educator John Dewey wrote:

> No permanent improvement in employment, and no genuine prosperity can be achieved, until state and local governments and particularly municipal governments, abandon their shortsighted taxing policies, and raise at least the major part of their budgets by taxing land values, so enabling them to exempt from taxation buildings, other labor products, machinery and stocks of goods, and personal property.[1]

The first chapter in this section describes a sample of land tax applications in the United States. The next chapter focuses on experiences with land value recapture in other countries. The final

155

chapter in this section looks at the impact of taxation on resources, contrasting the different end results in places that vigorously tax the value of raw resources and in places that do not.

———————————

NOTE

1. Dewey called George "one of the world's great social philosophers, certainly the greatest which this country has produced." See G. Geiger, Foreword, *The Philosophy of Henry George*, Macmillan, New York, 1933.

28

U.S. Success Stories

A NUMBER OF PLACES in the United States have chosen to test the healing power of taxing common property more and private property less. In so doing, they have reduced or overcome critical problems that have been troubling most regions and urban areas. Their experiences should engage the attention of economists, the media, and political leaders. The accounts are listed chronologically, based on when the land tax or land value recapture regimen was initiated.

Land Tax Applications Described in this Chapter

1887 California Irrigation Districts
1894 Fairhope, Alabama
1900 Arden, Delaware
1901 Cleveland, Ohio
1913 Pittsburgh, Pennsylvania
1918 New York City
1929 Miami (Ohio) Conservancy
1950 Rosslyn, Virginia
1960 Southfield, Michigan
1987 Peoria, Illinois

Other Pennsylvania Cities:
1975 Harrisburg
1977 Alliquippa
1982 New Castle
1985 Washington
1997 Allentown

Turning Water into Gold – *California Irrigation Districts*

After the Gold Rush, continental railroads and land hunger pro-
pelled waves of migrants westward to California. As population
there grew, so did the pressure to bring precious water to the state's
fertile but arid lands. Irrigation systems were built and it seemed
rational to charge farmers according to how much water they used.

This turned out to be unfair for the following reason. Small
farmers, to make a living, had no choice but to use great quantities
of water to grow fruits and vegetables on most of their dry acres.
Wealthy owners, on the other hand, let cattle and horses run over
their large ranches and used minimal amounts of water because they
did not use their lands intensively. Those in charge of financing the
irrigation districts noticed that the poorer growers bore most of
the cost of the dams and canals, whereas rich landowners paid
little, all the while their holdings were growing more valuable by
virtue of the presence of the irrigation systems.

To correct this inequity, California's Wright Act of 1887 specified
that all properties within an irrigation district should be taxed
according to their property value to support the projects. This
applied not only to farmland but also to town sites on the premise
that their value was enhanced by the greater productivity of
irrigated farms surrounding them.

The Wright Act was amended in 1909 to *permit*, and again in
1917 to *require*, that the tax fall on land values only, not on homes,
buildings, vineyards, crops, orchards, or other improvements. This
not only proved equitable, but in 1922 it enabled the Modesto and
Turlock irrigation districts to construct the Don Pedro Dam, at that
time the world's tallest, and it did so without a penny of state or
federal aid.

Land taxation turned water into gold in more ways than one.
Owners of huge ranches, under pocketbook pressures from the new
tax, began selling off their idle lands. The smaller tracts became
among the most intensively used and productive farm operations in
America.[1]

Land reformers around the world could have avoided failures and
violence had they followed this Wright way to more fairly distribute land. The incentives inherent in the land tax tend to automatically make land more accessible. Land reformers who used police

powers to confiscate and redistribute land to the landless stirred up social turmoil and rarely achieved durable land tenure systems to meet the needs of small farmers.

Even elsewhere in California, the Wright lessons were not followed. In the Central Valley and Feather River irrigation districts, landholders reaped the benefits but shifted the cost of dams and related infrastructure to state and federal taxpayers, who shelled out billions of dollars worth of subsidies to them.

Starting New Societies – *Fairhope and Arden*

Americans in the 19th Century founded intentional communities to fashion their own small societies in accord with their highest ideals. In this tradition, a number of Henry George followers tried to create land tax enclaves. These settlements, along with Utopian communities of other stripes, mostly fell by the wayside.[2]

Fairhope, Alabama, founded in 1894, long operated as a successful enclave on 4,000 acres. It grew from 25 people initially to some 17,000 by the year 2000. The Fairhope Single Tax Corporation leased land to residents and businesses, charging them only for their land value. This brought in enough revenue for the corporation to pay the taxes levied by Baldwin County, which were based on the conventional combined value of buildings plus land. Leftover surplus revenues were sufficient to enable the corporation to build excellent amenities – among them, a boat pier on Mobile Bay, water works, parks, schools, and a public library.

In the late 1900s population growth burgeoned alongside the colony. Many Fairhope residents envied new neighbors who were enriched by the area's booming land values. As a result, Fairhope officials, no longer imbued with the economic understanding or fervor of the founders, started to base leases on building values as well as land values. A minority of dedicated Georgists have been waging an uphill struggle to restore the original scheme.

Arden, founded north of Wilmington, Delaware in 1900, remains truer to its founding land tax principles. A popular haven for writers, artists and actors, the town added Ardentown and Ardencroft to accommodate more people. Residents with 99-year leases pay taxes to the community corporation based only on their individual land values and with no charges for the value of their homes. As in Fairhope, the community then pays conventional property taxes to the overlapping New Castle County, a necessary contortion to conform to state law. A popular dinner theater attracts visitors and residents enjoy a unique community spirit and neighborliness. The Ardens are attractive and persist as a demonstration that George's ideas work.[3]

Civic Revival – *Cleveland*

Tom L. Johnson, Cleveland's mayor from 1901 to 1909, made his city an exemplar of clean government and equality of opportunity at a time when cities across the nation were marked by corruption, favoritism, and bossism. *Progress and Poverty* convinced Johnson that special privileges and anti-competitive businesses were undermining cities. A former steel and railway monopolist himself, his inside knowledge made him an effective foe of monopolies.[4]

Once in office, Johnson instituted reforms that gave property owners fair and accurate assessments. His appraisal expert, John A. Zangerle, set what remains the gold standard for modern assessment administration. Johnson and Zangerle showed Clevelanders humongous assessment maps in public tent meetings to let all property owners see that they were being treated on the same basis as their neighbors.

At a time when cities were plagued by piles of stinking garbage that private firms were slow to pick up, Johnson gave Cleveland the nation's first city-owned trash collection unit. He put electric plants under city ownership as well. He took on the street railway owners and instituted a popular three-cent fare. He ordered humane treatment rather than imprisonment of vagrants. Unlike politicians who denounced liquor, saloons, and petty vice, Johnson worked to change the miserable conditions, like those Upton Sinclair portrayed in *The Jungle,* that drove people to drink or worse.

Lincoln Steffens, a noted social critic, singled out Cleveland as one of the rare exceptions to the corruption, cronyism, and mismanagement that characterized large cities. Johnson attracted and developed co-workers of integrity and ability who rose to national prominence – among them, Newton D. Baker, Frederick C. Howe, Brand Whitlock, Herbert S. Bigelow, and Peter Witt. Together that team of practical idealists demonstrated that cities can achieve greatness by freeing citizens and business from the clutches of special privilege.

Johnson's successors let his reforms fall by the wayside. Cleveland is now struggling. It was hit especially hard by the recession because of an excessive amount of "flipping". This was the practice by mortgage lenders to encourage realtors, including some with few assets, to buy properties and immediately sell them at higher prices. The flippers got cover for this kind of gambling as long as land values continued to rise, but their house of cards collapsed when the land bubble burst.

Cleveland's political and civic leaders would do well to reconsider Johnson's practices and principles to ignite a revitalization of their city.

Pioneering a Gradual Tax Shift – *Pittsburgh*

A method of gradually changing the conventional property tax to a modified land tax began in Pittsburgh in 1913. Republican Mayor William A. Magee, the prime mover, was inspired by Henry George. He won permission from the State Legislature to tax land and buildings at different rates. Each year the city slightly reduced its building tax rate and simultaneously slightly increased its tax rate on land values. After ten years, land was taxed at double the rate on homes and other improvements.

This reform spurred impressive new construction that continued even during the Depression. The tax change also touched off the post-World War II renaissance of the Golden Triangle, the downtown area wedged between the confluence of the Allegheny and Monongahela Rivers. David Lawrence,[5] mayor from 1946 to 1959, stressed the "stick" of the two-rate tax – the higher land tax pressured people to use sites to their full potential. Joseph M. Barr, mayor from 1959 to 1970, stressed the "carrot" – very low taxes on improvements encouraged construction and rehab.

When federal officials in the 1960s were designing a program to revive cities, they often cited Pittsburgh as their model. Those officials looked at the results but not at the carrot-and-stick of local tax reform that facilitated Pittsburgh's success. The federal urban renewal program fell far short of its high ambitions because it ignored tax incentives and relied instead on public subsidies, a prime example of economists whose mis-education blinded them to the critical role of land policy.

Allegheny County and the countywide school district both levied taxes on Pittsburgh properties. But these overlapping jurisdictions used the conventional form with no differential tax rates on land and buildings. Because of this, at the time of our Douglas Commission hearings there, Pittsburghers' *total* property tax (city, county, and school tax combined) had been whittled down from a 2-to-1 land-to-building ratio to a 5-to-4 ratio.

In 1979 the city, under the leadership of Councilman William J. Coyne, increased its differential to 3-to-l, then 4-to-1, and 6-to-1. Opponents predicted this would drive businesses away and hurt homeowners. They were mistaken. The change actually sparked what became known as Renaissance II. Corporate headquarters proliferated and handsome skyscrapers replaced outmoded structures and surface parking lots. Health and educational facilities expanded rapidly, softening the loss of the waning steel industry. National surveys put Pittsburgh in the top rank of cities with affordable housing. In the decade after adopting the 6-to-1 ratio, the dollar value of city building permits rose 70 percent while thirteen similar Rust Belt cities saw declines (see Table 2). Local newspaper editorials applauded the fact that the higher the land-to-building ratio of the tax rates, the more fine developments graced the city.

These good things came to a halt in 2000. An outside appraisal firm, hired to update assessments, focused only on *total* property values and so completely ignored land and improvement distinctions with the result that site values of identical adjacent parcels were valued miles apart. This upset taxpayers and threw a monkey wrench into the land tax. Confused city officials threw up their hands and reverted to the conventional property tax. For the best part of a century, Pittsburgh was America's prime demonstration of the practical benefits of shifting taxes off buildings and on to land. Letting property assessments become outdated and inaccurate brought this demonstration to an abrupt halt.

Pittsburgh's Business Improvement District, serving the central downtown area, continues to finance its projects by charging all properties within the district on the basis of their land values only. This remnant of the Georgist approach remains. Land tax proponents are working to restore the touchstone of Pittsburgh's former prominence on the urban stage.

TABLE 2

Growth and Decline in Rust Belt Cities
Comparing Pittsburgh and 14 Other Midwest Cities

Pittsburgh in 1979 significantly lowered taxes on buildings and increased them on land values. Rates on assessed building values were reduced to one-sixth the rates on assessed land values. All other cities in this study used the conventional property tax – one rate on the total building and land value. University of Maryland economists Wallace E. Oates and Robert M. Schwab tracked annual changes in new construction during the 1980s as compared with the prior two decades.

AVERAGE ANNUAL VALUE OF BUILDING PERMITS
Data for Central Cities, Values in Millions of Constant 1982 Dollars

	1960-79	1980-89	% Change
PITTSBURGH	**$181.734**	**$309.727**	**+70.43%**
Akron	$134.026	$87.907	-34.41%
Allentown	$48.124	$28.801	-40.15%
Buffalo	$93.749	$82.930	-11.54%
Canton	$40.235	$24.251	-39.73%
Cincinnati	$318.248	$231.561	-27.24%
Cleveland	$329.511	$224.587	-31.84%
Columbus	$456.580	$527.026	+15.43%
Dayton	$107.798	$92.249	-14.42%
Detroit	$368.894	$277.783	-24.70%
Erie	$48.353	$22.761	-52.93%
Rochester	$118.726	$82.411	-30.59%
Syracuse	$94.503	$53.673	-43.21%
Toledo	$138.384	$93.495	-32.44%
Youngstown	$33.688	$11.120	-66.99%
15-CITY AVERAGE	**$167.504**	**$143.352**	**-14.42%**

DATA: From Dun and Bradstreet. Based on Table 3 from Oates and Schwab, *The Impact of Urban Land Taxation: The Pittsburgh Experience*, Lincoln Institute for Land Policy, Cambridge, MA, 1992.

NOTE: Columbus is the only central city in this study besides Pittsburgh that showed a construction gain during the decade. Officials, in conversation with W. Rybeck, attributed this to the extensive annexations by Columbus during the 1980s. That city's data thus reflect building expansion in former suburbs surrounding the central city.

Easing a Housing Crisis – *New York City*

New York City faced an acute housing shortage after World War I. Sensing that high building taxes were impeding development, the city won permission from the State Legislature to exempt taxes on new apartment buildings for ten years. Land beneath the buildings continued to be taxed. This reform immediately touched off a building boom, erasing the shortage of dwelling units and boosting municipal revenue. The $83 million worth of exempted housing the first year kept growing to over $900 million by the sixth year, for a cumulative total of $3.4 billion worth of new construction.

The housing supply crisis had ended. Builders understandably catered at first to the up-scale market. It was anticipated that continued exemptions would add to the supply of housing for middle and lower income tenants, bringing rents down. However, in 1926, powerful real estate speculators who were prevented by the land tax from cashing in on rising values persuaded the state and city to phase out the exemption program.

Instead of learning from that successful example, the city's subsequent housing specialists took the path of rent controls, subsidies to lenders and landlords, and public housing. Whatever the merits of these alternative approaches, long a matter of controversy, their results have not begun to match the impressive achievements of New York City's all-too-short land tax venture.[6]

Paying for Infrastructure – *Miami Conservancy of Ohio*

To pay for the system of dams built to prevent future floods in the Miami Valley of Ohio, Conservancy Director Arthur Morgan ordered a massive appraisal operation. The 77,000 properties along 110 miles of river valley were to be taxed on the basis of how much damage protection each parcel was receiving.[7] Damage protection was a proxy for each property's land value gain. It was politically palatable because it was easily recognized as a charge for the benefit being provided to each location. People who had suffered terrible flood losses readily agreed to bear the cost of avoiding a repetition of that disaster. The tax brought in more than enough revenue to pay for the dams and levees. Without federal, state, or local subsidy, site owners directly benefiting paid for the construction and operation of this major infrastructure project.

Unlike most taxes that deter or slow down development, Morgan's land tax scheme hastened an outstanding industrial and commercial revival throughout the Dayton region. This revenue device affirmed the theory that taxing the value of land encourages owners to make optimal use of the potential of their holdings.

Obeying the Law – *Rosslyn, Virginia, and Southfield, Michigan*

Exciting things happened when two local governments stopped under-assessing land and over-assessing the value of buildings. American assessors were typically assessing land and improvements improperly, documented in New York City and Dayton (see Chapter 15). Later studies by the Census of Governments, the Committee for Economic Development, and the Advisory Committee for Intergovernmental Relations all confirmed that this departure from market value evaluations was widespread.

Rosslyn, across the Potomac River from Washington, D.C., and Southfield, which shared a border with Detroit, began assessing land at its full current market value, a novel approach although it was nothing more than what the law specifies. The corrected assessments reduced taxes on buildings and raised them on land values, touching off impressive development in both communities.

Rosslyn instituted its reform when the area was an unsightly residential, commercial, and industrial slum, a jumble of pawn shops, lumber yards, warehouses, and junk yards. To picture the jolt landowners got from the reassessment, one five-acre commercial tract saw its appraised value rise from $3,000 to $196,000 an acre. A 154-acre industrial tract, formerly appraised at $300 an acre, saw an increase to $2,300 an acre. Owners, despite the derelict appearance of their sites, got a wake-up call that they were sitting on gold-plated locations. Confronted with an annual tax based on that fact, the owners promptly began using their sites appropriately or sold to others who were eager to locate there.

Within a few years of bringing land value assessments up to current market value, Rosslyn was transformed into a skyscraper city. It became filled with a wide range of enterprises and public agencies that provided employment to tens of thousands.[8]

Crossing the street from Detroit to Southfield, locals said, was like going from night to day. Before Southfield corrected its assessments, land was assessed at only 10 percent of its value while buildings were assessed at 70 to 85 percent of value. After the city initiated a robust taxation of land values, new buildings and new enterprises began to appear. Despite higher land taxes, average homeowners enjoyed a 22 percent reduction in their property taxes. Reduced taxes on their buildings more than compensated for their higher site taxes.[9]

In contrast, Detroit, next door to Southfield, barely taxed land values and put the weight of the property tax on structures. As Southfield prospered, Detroit went into an economic tailspin.

For cities with property assessments that deviate from the legal requirements, the moral of the Rosslyn and Southfield stories is clear. *Simply obeying the law* is an easily accomplished and important first reform of the property tax. It is not a land tax, but it is a beneficial change in the right direction.

A further lesson can be drawn from Detroit's malaise. Like Cleveland in the Progressive era, Detroit had a Georgist mayor, Hazen Pingree. He raised land taxes, which played no small part in enabling Detroit to become the auto-making capital of the world.[10] Detroit outpaced the growth rate of all American cities, becoming the nation's fourth largest by 1950. Subsequent governors, however, began instituting income, business, and corporate taxes in the name of "property tax relief". In 1995 Michigan hastened the decline of Detroit, Flint, and other cities by deciding to use sales taxes instead of property taxes to finance public education. Taxing enterprise helped kill Detroit's golden goose.[11]

Still Going Strong – *Pennsylvania*

Before Pittsburgh's reassessment debacle led the city to abandon its two-rate tax, many other cities in the state had gotten aboard the land tax bandwagon. Much credit goes to Stephen Cord, a professor in Pennsylvania's Indiana University, the Johnny Appleseed of the reform movement. He traveled the state, giving local officials nuts-and-bolts recipes for making property taxes more equitable. Joshua Vincent, who succeeded Cord as director of the Center for the Study of Economics, continues to provide technical help to localities that are modernizing their property taxes.

Pennsylvania cities that adopted the two-rate tax kept housing prices stable while they soared elsewhere in the state and nation. Most home and apartment owners enjoyed property tax reductions. New construction and rehab expanded while they declined in comparable nearby cities. The tax change attracted private development, revitalizing central business districts. Tapping previously under-taxed land values increased municipal revenues. As idle lots and derelict buildings in the city were put back into use, sprawl was minimized.

Some skeptics attributed these good results to other local and national policy changes that occurred at the same time. Certainly, the land tax was only one of a kit of tools these cities used. Nevertheless, every city using the two-rate tax recorded positive results while their similar neighboring cities *that used those other tools but not the land tax*, stagnated. It strains credulity to dismiss the consistent tax reform benefits as coincidental. The land tax proved to be not only a constructive measure, but also a device that helped other urban strategies to become more effective.

Pennsylvania's two-rate taxing cities are not devoid of problems. Notably, most continue to impose onerous taxes on businesses and workers. Their small doses of land taxation nevertheless have achieved measurable gains – results that earn this reform the right to be labeled high-potency medicine. The army of urbanologists who have had minimal success in halting chronic city problems should ask: How much healthier would America's ailing cities be if they stopped taxing privately created values and relied to a much greater extent on recapturing publicly-created land values?

Harrisburg   Before the state capital initiated the two-rate tax, the U.S. Department of Housing and Urban Development listed Harrisburg (population 48,950) as the nation's second most distressed city of its size class. The city was in big trouble, having lost 800 businesses and a third of its population in the prior two decades.

The two-rate tax launched by Mayor Stephen Reed reversed the city's downward slide. All but a handful of its 5,200 stores and housing units that were boarded up when he took office were replaced or rehabilitated and put back into use within a decade. New construction up to the time of Reed's retirement in 2010 increased the city's taxable real estate from $212 million to over $1.6 billion. Businesses on the tax rolls rose from 1,908 to more than 2,100 by the year 2009.

The tax rate on land was first set at 2.6 times higher than the rate on buildings. As the City Council and citizens saw positive effects, they gradually increased the land rate to 6 times higher than the rate on improvements.

Mayor Reed explained the anti-sprawl effect of the reform as follows: "Unused urban land is what pushes development into open spaces. Many states try to save farmland by buying development rights. That's expensive. Without spending a dime, we achieved the same goal with our two-tier tax."

Aliquippa   When the LTV steel mill shut down, Aliquippa (population 13,400) lost its main industry and 15,000 jobs. The mill owners took their annual property tax bill of $1 million to court and got it reduced to $200,000. Aliquippa then moved to tax land values at a rate 16 times higher than on buildings. This shift of tax burdens onto land values rather than on improvements brought LTV's tax bill up to $450,000, a charge that gave the corporation an incentive to find new uses for its plant, which it accomplished quickly.

Within a couple years, Aliquippa's building permits increased 200 percent, four-fifths of its residents got tax reductions, city revenues increased 10 percent, and the town had a budget surplus.

New Castle   This western Pennsylvania city (population 28,300), during its first three years with a two-rate tax, saw 75 percent of its homeowners get property tax reductions. Seniors on fixed incomes, squeezed by steadily rising taxes, previously were being forced to leave their homes, friends, and familiar surroundings. With the two-rate tax they could afford to stay and their neighborhoods were stabilized. Even in the midst of a sharp recession, new downtown development occurred.

Washington   A short distance south of Pittsburgh, Washington (population 15,800) adopted the two-rate tax in 1985 in response to a court-ordered reassessment. Under the conventional U.S. property tax, the new assessments would have spelled tax increases for most homeowners. Under the two-rate tax, 85 percent paid lower taxes.

Mayor Anthony Spossey said the reform reversed three decades of decline, induced new construction, and turned the city's budget

TABLE 3

Two-Rate Taxing Jurisdictions in Pennsylvania as of 2009

TAX RATES ON LAND AND BUILDINGS
Compared to Rates under Conventional Property Tax
to Raise the Same Revenue

Jurisdiction	Land Tax Rate (in mills)[1]	Building Tax Rate (in mills)[2]	Tax Ratio[3]	Property Tax Rate (in mills)[4]	Year adopted
Aliquippa School District	188.000	29.500	6.4	60.530	1993
Aliquippa City	81.000	11.400	7.1	24.900	1988
Allentown City	50.380	10.720	4.7	17.520	1997
Altoona City	185.860	6.890	27.0	30.000	2002
Clairton City	28.000	2.220	12.6	7.500	1989
Clairton School District	75.000	3.100	24.2	22.000	2006
DuBois City	89.000	3.000	29.7	1870	1991
Duquesne City	19.000	13.470	1.4	8.050	1985
Ebensburg Borough	27.500	7.500	3.7	10.500	2000
Harrisburg City	28.670	4.780	6.0	9.630	1975
Lock Haven City	16.260	2.950	5.5	6.289	1991
McKeesport City	16.500	4.260	3.9	11.260	1980
New Castle City	27.791	7.856	3.5	11.726	1982
Pittsburgh Improvement District	4.374	N/A	N/A	N/A	1997
Scranton City	103.145	22.432	4.6	28.500	1913
Titusville City	53.510	13.35	4.0	18.333	1990
Washington City	100.630	3.500	28.8	21.620	1985

NOTES

1 Information provided by the Center for the Study of Economics, Philadelphia, Pa.

2 In Pennsylvania, tax rates are expressed in mills. A mill is 1/1000th of a dollar.

3 Column 3, the tax ratio is column 1 divided by column 2. In the Aliquippa School District, for instance, the figure means that the land tax rate is over 6 times higher than the rate on buildings. This column shows that Altoona and three other jurisdictions get most property tax revenue from land, with only token amounts from buildings.

4 Column 4 indicates what the conventional property tax rate would need to be to raise the identical total revenue generated by the two-rate tax.

from red to black. Building permits from 1987 through 1995 totaled a hefty $22 million – roughly one-third for residential structures, and two-thirds for commercial and industrial buildings.

Allentown   Few large landholders speak out against land taxes. They prefer to persuade folks like old ladies in tennis shoes to front for them and make it appear "little people" will suffer from tax reform. Allentown (population 107,000) had an outspoken promoter of land speculation who was the exception to this rule.

The late Donald Miller, publisher of the *Allentown Call*, was also a parking mogul. His surface lots had some ten thousand car spaces. So many buildings in the central business district were torn down for his lots that it was hard to find businesses. Miller was powerful enough to persuade the mayor to veto two-rate tax ordinances year after year, although City Council persevered and finally won in 1997.

Miller's forthright arguments illustrated a mind set against reform. When Councilman Ben Howells began pushing the land tax in 1982, here is a sample of what Miller wrote in his newspaper: "*Land speculation has been an American practice since the Pilgrims came to the New World in 1620. Laws will not change this practice because every American dreams of a quick kill on real estate if he has the foresight to buy land at locations that will command a profit.*"

Miller deserved a prize for candor. But his praise of "quick kills" by speculators at society's expense should motivate champions of urban progress to oppose that tactic.

Implications of the Numbers

Walking through examples of the tax rates in Table 3 as they apply to four different types of property in Washington, Pennsylvania, clarifies how the two-rate tax differs from the typical property tax.

Note that the following examples illustrate how the old conventional property tax favors poor land use – or no use – while the two-rate tax favors homeowners and business owners who make good use of their properties. When most of the tax falls on the land value, as in Washington, Clairton, Altoona, and Dubois, the sizeable percentage increases in the annual tax on idle lands gives owners of those sites a considerable wake-up call to put their holdings to better use.

1. A fine, well maintained residence. Land assessed at $10,000, house at $90,000

		column in $s	
TYPICAL OLD PROPERTY TAX	total assessed value	= 100,000	
Tax rate, 21.62 mills,	tax bill, $100,000 x .02162		= **2,162**
UNDER TWO-RATE TAX	land tax, $10,000 x .10063		= 1,006
	building tax, $90.000 x .0035		= 315
	total tax bill	= **1,321**	
Owner's SAVING	38.9% a year LESS or		= 841

2. A boarded-up, blighted apartment. Land assessed at $120,000, building at $50,000

UNDER OLD PROPERTY TAX	total assessed value	=170,000	
Tax rate, 21.62 mills,	tax bill, $170,000 x .02162		= 3,675
UNDER TWO-RATE TAX	land tax, $120,000 x .10063		= 12,076
	building tax, $50.000 x .0035		= 175
	total tax bill	= **12,251**	
Owner's INCREASE	233% a year MORE or		= 8,576

3. A highly-developed business site. Land assessed at $300,000, building at $1,800,000

UNDER OLD PROPERTY TAX	total assessed value	=2,100,000	
Tax rate, 21.62 mills,	tax bill, $2,100,000 x .02162		= **45,402**
UNDER TWO-RATE TAX	land tax, $300,000 x .10063		= 30,189
	building tax, $1,800,000 x .0035		= 6,300
	total tax bill	= **36.489**	
Owner's SAVING	19.6% a year LESS or		= 8,913

4. An empty lot in central business district. Land assessed at $250,000, no improvements

UNDER OLD PROPERTY TAX	total assessed value	=250,000	
Tax rate, 21.62 mills,	tax bill, $250,000 x .02162		= 5,405
UNDER TWO-RATE TAX	land tax, $250,000 x .10063		= 25,158
	building tax (no building)		= 0
	total tax bill	= **25,158**	
Owner's INCREASE	365% a year MORE or		= 19,753

How Did Reform Play – *Peoria*

Peoria won a reputation as the prototypical Middle American small city, so much so that firms testing new products and politicians airing new policies would ask, "How will it play in Peoria?"

Land value taxation played well in Peoria's run-down industrial area along the Illinois River. A derelict seven-mile-long strip of obsolete factories and warehouses was so blighted that a plan to simply bulldoze everything was seriously proposed. The area employed only 2,000 people in the 1980s, down from 50,000 in its heyday six decades earlier.

Under the Illinois Enterprise Zone law, taxes on new improvements were reduced 75 percent for five years, 50 percent for the next five. These reductions applied only to the value of new or renovated buildings, not to the land under them. Taxes on each parcel increased as its site value rose. After this plan was adopted, activity in the area mushroomed. Within a few years the dollar value of industrial-commercial building permits within the zone rose dramatically from 8 percent to 29 percent of the citywide total.[12]

The private market works when conditions are favorable. Many city leaders fail to see that failure to create a favorable tax climate saps enterprise or drives it away. As their cities suffer a downward spiral, officials and city planners then try to act like developers, putting together real estate deals, either on their own or via private-public partnerships. When officials launch arenas and large commercial centers, often of a showy nature, they are lauded for giving cities a boost, but these projects rarely turn the local economy around. Cities also entice new ventures to locate there, using as bait costly concessions and grants (paid for by taxing older local enterprises and putting them at a competitive disadvantage). Not infrequently the subsidized newcomers use up their grants and then disappear into the night.

The enlightened business people who devised Peoria's land tax observed that some local officials and planners opposed the plan because it gave them no goodies to bargain with, no new powers, and no ability to pick economic winners and losers. According to proponents, city leaders finally approved the tax reform, not because they thought it would work but because they were fairly sure it would not.

Notes

1. This did not happen without opposition. Big landowners, banks, and utilities viciously fought the Wright Act through the courts, labeling it "communism ... under the guise of law". The U.S. Supreme Court, disagreeing, upheld the act.
2. Among enclaves founded by land tax promoters but that failed to install or retain a land tax system were Tahanto, Shakerton, and Trapelo in Massachusetts, Halidon in Maine, and Free Acres in New Jersey.
3. Henry Wiencek called Arden "an oasis of idiosyncrasy", *Smithsonian Magazine*, May 1992.
4. Johnson's autobiography, *My Story*, New York, 1911. He writes that Henry George persuaded him to fight for economic justice. Johnson's statue in Cleveland's center square shows him holding George's famous book.
5. Lawrence became Pennsylvania Governor, 1959-63, and chaired the Equal Housing Opportunity Committee under Presidents Kennedy and Johnson.
6. "How Tax Exemption Broke the Housing Deadlock in New York City", preface by W. Rybeck, Citizens' Housing and Planning Council of New York, New York City, 1960.
7. For more about Morgan and his Ohio flood protection system, see Chapter 10.
8. Lyle C. Bryant, "Rosslyn: A Case Study in Urban Renewal", American University, D.C., 1967.
9. Southfield Mayor James Clarkson, "Hearing Before the National Commission on Urban Problems", Vol. 5, Government Printing Office, Washington, D.C., 1967, pp.36-45.
10. Later, as Michigan's governor, Pingree centralized the state's assessment administration. His staff found so much untaxed land that Michigan was able to reduce tax rates and bring in increased revenues at the same time.
11. A detailed account of this sorry tale is given by Mason Gaffney, "What's the Matter with Michigan: Rise and Collapse of an Economic Wonder", in *GroundSwell*, Beloit, WI, December 2008.
12. The county, city, school district, park district, transit district and other entities that had to sign off on the plan did not let the new tax regimen apply to either residential or retail uses.

29

Overseas
Success Stories

"The land tax as the only means of supporting the government is an infinitely just, reasonable, and equitably distributed tax."
— Sun Yat Sen,
founder of modern, pre-Communist China

WHILE HENRY GEORGE'S proposals were being belittled in his native country, other nations put his prescription for social justice to the test with excellent results. The reliance on land-based revenue sources by Hong Kong and New Zealand actually predated George, showing that he had no patent on this approach. It is associated with him because his explanations and justifications for it were far more extensive than those of other economists or political scientists before or since.

To sample foreign examples of land value collection, we look at the following countries, listed by the year they adopted that policy:

    1843 Hong Kong
    1878 New Zealand
    1912 Denmark
    1916 South Africa
    1949 Taiwan

174

Half-Told Story – *Hong Kong*

The late Milton Friedman and the late Jack Kemp frequently cited Hong Kong as an example of the good results stemming from the low-tax policies they advocated.

When Hong Kong was still a British colony and before mainland China took control, anti-taxers credited the economic miracle of this bustling outpost in Asia to several facts: dividends, capital gains, and sales were not taxed; progressive salary taxes ranged from only 2 to 25 percent, but with a ceiling of 15 percent of gross income; and, as of 1996, generous personal allowances kept 44 percent of the labor force from paying any income taxes at all.

This account was true, as far as it went. However, low-tax proponents failed to wonder or ask how Hong Kong avoided onerous taxes on wage earners and businesses and yet afforded to continuously upgrade roads, transit, harbor, airports, parks, and so forth. Anyone who has read to this point will guess correctly that Hong Kong generated the bulk of its revenue from land values. The colony did this in spades, recapturing 40 percent of Hong Kong's rapidly expanding land values during the two decades after 1970 when these values soared to unprecedented heights.[1]

Hong Kong owned virtually all its land and the colony leased these "crown lands". Lease contracts did not keep pace with sky-rocketing land values, so it became profitable for leaseholders to sublease. In response, Hong Kong imposed a high profits tax on these subleases.

It is important to note that there is no *economic* difference between paying the government *rent* for a lease on *publicly owned land* and paying the government a *tax* on *privately owned land*. There are many *political* differences, however, and to my mind there are many advantages in the private ownership system that predominates in America.

Should Hong Kong be defined as a low-tax or high-tax example? Both. It imposes low taxes of the type that tend to suppress an economy – on income, dividends, and sales. It has prospered by imposing high charges in the form of rents and taxes on land values. In sum, it may be said that Hong Kong has high and low taxes of the right kinds.

Postcard and Pocketbook Politics – *New Zealand*

To acquaint Americans with flourishing land tax governments abroad, V.G. Peterson, executive director of the Schalkenbach Foundation, arranged national tours of prominent foreign spokesmen from those countries.[2] I helped arrange some of their speaking engagements and thus became acquainted with Rolland O'Regan of New Zealand, Viggo Starcke of Denmark, and Frank A.W. Lucas of South Africa.

Dr Rolland O'Regan, besides being a land tax reformer, was one of New Zealand's leading surgeons, an executive of his nation's Labour Party, a Wellington City Councilman who chaired the Town Planning Committee, and Deputy President of the Royal Forest and Bird Protection Society.

Addressing a George Washington University faculty meeting in Washington, he reported that 293 of New Zealand's 367 cities, boroughs, and counties had adopted a property tax based on land values alone, with no tax on homes or other structures. How, he was asked, was such an extensive change engineered?

He said reformers first generated support among citizens to petition their jurisdictions to hold polls on whether to adopt a land tax. Next they collected the official data on land and improvement assessments for every parcel. From this data they calculated the taxes due under both the old and the proposed systems and sent this information on a postcard to each owner. Only property owners were entitled to vote in these polls. Because a majority saw they would pay less when homes and other buildings were no longer taxed, favorable votes occurred time and again around the country.[3]

A lesson from the New Zealand experience is that success in the political arena requires paying close attention to the pocketbook impacts of the reform. Ethical considerations and careful economic analyses were instrumental in motivating leaders of the reform. However, they took pains to translate their proposals so all taxpayers could answer the question that inevitably arises when a major change is being debated: "If this reform passes, how will it affect *me*?"

Folk Schools and Land Taxes – *Denmark*

Viggo Starcke, Danish author and historian, was a Member of Parliament in the Justice Party, a party dedicated to land taxation, free markets, and free trade. When the Justice Party became part of a ruling coalition, Starcke as party leader served as minister without portfolio in the Danish Government from 1957 to 1960. It was during that period that he made his U.S. tour.

According to Starcke, George's *Progress and Poverty* struck a familiar chord with Danes because Valdemar the Great in the 12th Century instituted a land tax that led to several centuries of good times and progress for Denmark. However, by the 1800s many Danes were reduced to near serfdom on huge baronial estates.

The Danish Folk School movement, founded by Bishop Severin Grundtvig, taught Henry George's ideas to landless farmers. In the early 1900s Danish peasant farmers were having bad times. They marched on Copenhagen and puzzled officials by saying they wanted no charity, no protective tariffs, no relief or special privileges – only land value taxation. Parliament first tried some different tax policies that worked poorly, but in 1912 they adopted a national land tax.

Owners of large estates, to avoid the higher taxes, started selling off land they were not using. Within a generation, Starcke said, Denmark had become a country of intensively used and highly productive smaller farms, winning fame for the little nation as "the breadbasket of Europe".

Speaking in American churches, Starcke gave a memorable sermon on "Our Daily Bread". He took out tiny bread loaves from his pocket, creatively using them to illustrate different economic systems and to reveal why property is sometimes rightfully *mine*, at other times *yours*, and in still other circumstances *ours*.[4]

Land Tax and Apartheid – *South Africa*

Frank A.W. Lucas, a justice of South Africa's high court, reported that a 1916 law enabled cities in his country to tax property according to site value alone. Johannesburg and nearly a hundred other cities adopted this reform. Surveys by Godfrey Dunkley, an internationally esteemed appraiser in South Africa, found that over a twenty-year period the site value cities attracted double the capital growth of cities using their old system, which is comparable to the typical U.S. property tax.

For those inclined to be pessimistic about the prospects for social change in general, or land tax reform in particular, another aspect of Lucas's visit is pertinent. He came to an America where segregation was widespread and when lynching of blacks still occurred. Lucas wore a black armband in mourning for the blacks in his country who had just been expelled from "white areas" and jammed into special enclaves under the *apartheid* policy. The judge pronounced it apart-*hate*.

At that time people who were considered authorities on South Africa did not debate whether that nation was headed for a bloodbath. They only disagreed on how soon it would happen. Anyone surely would have been accused of living in a fantasy world if he or she had predicted then that Nelson Mandela, a black man about to be imprisoned, would emerge 27 years later to resolve South Africa's racial divide in a peaceful and healing manner. It would have sounded even more preposterous if someone had predicted at that time that Lucas's U.S. audiences, half a century later, would help elect a black president.

Unlikely outcomes such as these should give hope to those working for a more just society.

Georgist Constitution – *Taiwan*

Sun Yat Sen, leader of the new China republic in the early 1900s, proclaimed that profits arising from increased land values should accrue to all the people, not a privileged few. Discussing his plans with American journalists, he said, "The teaching of your single taxer, Henry George, will be the basis of our program of reform."[5]

Chiang Kai-shek, who assumed leadership in the 1920s, did not pursue Sun Yat Sen's policy. He chose not to buck the powerful landowners of his own Kuomintang party. In addition, he was busy fighting Communist rivals. But the wars – China's civil war and World War II – led to a strange turn of events.

After his defeat by the Communists in 1949, Chiang fled with remnants of his followers to set up an alternative Republic of China on the island of Taiwan. Landlords there were no longer *his* landlords, and Chiang conveniently recalled Sun Yat Sen's ideas about land. More than simply remembering, he and his regime spelled out the land ethic in Article 143 of Taiwan's constitution, to provide the following:

- Privately owned land shall be liable to taxation according to its value.
- Government may buy land according to its assessed value. (Taiwanese owners declare the value of their own land; the government's right to purchase at that value keeps people from setting self-assessments too low.)
- If the value of a parcel is increased, not due to the exertion of labor or use of capital, that increase shall be subject to an increment tax, the proceeds of which shall be enjoyed by the people in common.

The land tax generated four times more revenue for Taiwan than its separate tax on homes. Rates for the *graduated* tax levied on land value increments went up in multiples. If the land value of a parcel increased 100 percent, the government taxed 40 percent of that. For increases between 100 and 200 percent, the tax was 50 percent. Increases from 200 to 300 percent were taxed at 60 percent. Over thirty years, the revenue generated by land taxes increased more than 600,000 percent. (Not a misprint!)

Impacts of the land tax on this small poverty-stricken island less than the size of West Virginia were impressive. From 1950 to 1990, the country changed from a net importer to a net exporter. Taiwan attained world power status. Its gross national product or GNP during that period rose from $1.2 billion to $150 billion, expressed in U.S. dollars. While the farming sector prospered, industrial growth so greatly outpaced it that, in this same time period, agriculture declined from 33 percent to half of 1 percent of GNP.

Meanwhile, urban buildings increased 230 percent. In conjunction with other policies, the land tax helped keep development and industry within the confines of cities, saving scarce prime flatlands for agriculture.[6]

Et Cetera

Other examples that could be cited include many Australian cities, Singapore, parts of Canada, and Abu Dhabi.[7] A fair conclusion from a review of land tax implementation efforts is that their socio-economic impacts are beneficial. These benefits increase in direct proportion to the degree of reliance on taxing land values and, equally important, to the degree that the fruits of labor and production are relieved from taxation.

NOTES

1. Yu-Hung Hong, *Does Public Land Leasing Pay? Managing Public Land through Land Contracting in Hong Kong*, Lincoln Institute of Land Policy, Cambridge, MA, 1994.
2. The Robert Schalkenbach Foundation, formed in New York in 1926 to promote the works and ideas of Henry George, funds research and public education on land economics.
3. O'Regan's book, *Rating in New Zealand*, Barunduin Publishers, Wainuiomata, NZ, 1973, offers rare insights into appraisal technicalities and the framing of property tax laws. "Rating" is the term used for property taxation in New Zealand, Australia, and Britain.
4. Some main points of Starcke's sermon are excerpted in Appendix D.
5. Quoted in *The Republic*, Chicago, April 12, 1912.
6. Sein Lin, "Taiwan's Formula…" in W. Rybeck, ed., *From Poverty to Prosperity by 2000*, Center for Public Dialogue, Kensington, MD, 1992; and Arch Woodruff, president emeritus, University of Hartford, "Lessons from Taiwan", speech to International Conference at Woudschoten, Holland, July 1982.
7. Bookshelves of material on the history of these reforms are available. Robert V. Andelson, ed., *Land Value Taxation Around the World*, 3rd edition, Blackwell, Malden, Me., 2000, includes many references.

30

Taxing
Natural Resources

BECAUSE THE VALUES OF RESOURCES in the ground are more
mysterious to most of us than the values of surface lands on which
our homes and businesses are located, it is useful to look briefly at
some aspects of these natural resources.

The People's Share – *Alaska vs Appalachia*

Widely advertised is the fact that every Alaskan man, woman, and
child gets a sizeable annual dividend – amounting over a decade
to tens of thousands of dollars for a family – from the state's
Permanent Fund. The Fund, financed by oil, was established in 1976
and its rules, enshrined in the State Constitution, recognize the
distinctions between private and common property. As petroleum
economist Chuck Logsdon with the Department of Natural
Resources explained to me, "Private companies own the gas and oil
they extract; the Alaskan people get the land rent."

Private energy firms, far from being deterred by this policy,
eagerly compete for leases to tap the Alaska-owned petroleum
reserves. In return, they pay royalties, corporate taxes, severance
taxes, and property taxes. Citizens enjoy both monetary dividends
and low tax burdens because oil revenues cover a large portion of
state and local budgets.

Alaska presents a stark contrast with Appalachian states. They
too are well endowed with natural resources – oil, gas, coal,
timber, quarries. These states let corporations pocket not only their

legitimate earnings from their extraction activities, but also the common land values that belong to citizens of Appalachia. Lest the uninitiated think these land values are picayune, one Pennsylvania coal company sold its twelve Somerset County mines for $1.3 billion in 2008.

The failure to distinguish what belongs to the people and what belongs to the producers is a major cause of the chronic poverty which seems ludicrous in resource-rich states. Those states desperately need to take a lesson from Alaska's book.

Taxing Coal into Use

"I've got a prize for whoever tells me why a major coal operator asked the Ohio Legislature to raise his taxes."

My brother Art often opened talks about reviving West Virginia's economy with that question, noting that "Tax me, please," is not what the typical industrialist pleads for.

To start at the beginning of this story: in central West Virginia, Fayette County officials had prepared a modest bond issue to upgrade their schools. They were shocked when the issue was stricken from the ballot on grounds that local property values were insufficient to underwrite the bonds. They approached me to ask how this was possible since rich seams of coal underlay almost the entire county.

My inquiry began with a query to the assessor in Wheeling, my home town, about how he valued the coal of a local mining firm. "I go by what the company reports," was his unexpected reply. Off I went to the manager of that company, Valley Coal, to ask just what he reports to the assessor.

"Each year," he said, "we report how many acres of coal we extracted" to reduce the property being taxed. That seemed only fair. Coal that no longer exists should not be taxed. But I asked how he sets the value of the remaining inventory of coal still in the ground.

"Oh, we just don't challenge the rate that's been set," he replied.

The rate that's been set got to the crux of the issue. Mining almost ceased during the Great Depression. Simply to keep mine properties on the books, assessments were dropped to a token rate of around $5 an acre of coal. World War II and then the nation's hunger for the electricity produced from coal revived demand for "black gold". While production and profits soared, however, assessments remained static. It was obvious why coal owners did not challenge "the rate that's been set".

One operator, James Hyslop, who happened to be a dental patient of my brother's, did challenge "the rate that's been set". He managed coal operations in southeast Ohio for the Hanna Corporation. Coal in the ground, he told me, was worth "hundreds of times more" than the assessed value. "I decided to ask legislators in Columbus to raise taxes on my coal," he added.

"Why in the world did you do that?" I asked to elicit his reasoning.

Hanna, he explained, was a highly diversified corporation with many sources of income and no need for current profits from its extensive coal holdings. In fact, with minimal taxes on these holdings, he said the firm could afford to sit on them for another century, after which they would be worth far more.[1]

Hyslop nevertheless felt his mission was to maximize mining. After Ohio took his advice and assessed coal more realistically, Hanna ramped up production to offset its tax costs, just as Hyslop predicted. That was not the end of his story. More coal on the market brought its price down, letting it out-compete other energy sources. Hyslop's coal division created many new jobs. Moreover – the answer I was looking for – cities and counties where the firm operated were able, with increased coal tax revenues, to provide decent schools, police protection, and roads.

With Hyslop's permission, I repeated his story in a deposition for Fayette County. John O. Behrens, one of the nation's specialists on property tax law, joined me to buttress the case. He emphasized that the law requires assessors to value coal on the same basis as residential and other business properties, that is, at current market value. That's common sense, but not common practice.

Poor Rich Appalachia

The U.S. Supreme Court took a turn that retarded fair assessments of coal in West Virginia.[2]

Sales revealing the true worth of coal lands are quite rare because their low assessments make it financially painless to hold on to them. So it was noteworthy when the Allegheny-Pittsburgh Coal Company paid $24 million in 1975 for a parcel in Webster County that contained an estimated 32 million tons of coal. The company sold it seven years later to East Kentucky Energy Corp. for $30 million.

County Assessor Stanis Morton, noting these prices, appraised the property accordingly.[3] The owners cried foul, saying they were assessed far higher than neighboring coal fields. West Virginia's high court did not dispute the disparity but supported Morton for using a market value test as the law required. The state court defended him from a charge of discrimination by pointing to three years in which he raised assessments on other coal holdings.

When the case landed in the U.S. Supreme Court, Chief Justice Charles Rehnquist countered that, at the rate these adjustments were being made, it would take 500 years before the neighbors' assessments were brought up to a par with the Allegheny/East Kentucky valuations.

Did the court therefore rule that West Virginia obey its law and bring *all* coal valuations up to a fair level? No, instead of holding assessors' feet to the fire, the Supreme Court in a unanimous decision required Webster County to repay the coal company for its excess tax payments. Did the governor or state legislature then do what the justices may have felt was beyond their purview and correct the system? Again, no. Morton's successor, Assessor Dana Lynch, said the state then took coal evaluation from counties and gave the job to the state assessing office which, as of 2010, still had not gotten around to mapping and evaluating the rich coal remaining in the seams under Webster County.

Court testimony indicated the actual value of coal was 3,500 percent higher than it was being valued for tax purposes. One must wonder how many billions of dollars of tax revenue were forgone, billions that could have helped ease the severe poverty in West Virginia's cities, towns, and rural areas. These billions went instead to the absentee owners who control the state's natural resources.[4]

Where was West Virginia's next-generation James Hyslop when they needed him – a progressive manager who knew how to strengthen the mining industry and the public sector respectively?

THE 'CURSE' OF RESOURCES

Is it not puzzling and strange, I asked, that West Virginia, so rich in coal, natural gas, oil, and timber is so poverty-ridden?

"It's not strange," the late James Busey replied. A Colorado political science professor and Latin America specialist, he said, "This is the usual fate of places cursed with natural resources." He explained that resources lure exploiters who often go the next step and corrupt government, giving top officials a slice of their plunder in exchange for subjugating the mass of the population.

Busey, of course, used the word "cursed" ironically. He agreed that resources *should* be a blessing, and *could be* if subjected to a more equitable tax system. In Alaska, the public taps the value of resources in their natural state and leaves to enterprisers the values they add through extraction, refinement, and distribution – so both the industry and the general population thrive.

Strike Charade

Early in my reporting days in Fairmont, in 1947, the national press was relating that the coal miners under the fiery United Mine Workers chief, John L. Lewis in Washington, were locked in a bitter battle with the coal owners. The large concentration of bituminous coal miners were represented by UMW District 50 in Fairmont. Consolidated Coal, the largest coalfield operator, was also headquartered in Fairmont.

"Don't fall for this so-called coal war," said a man I interviewed. He claimed the leaders of District 50 and Consol were "lunch buddies" waging a sham fight. Just wait, he said, and you will see that they let the union claim victory with higher wages. The companies will use that as an excuse to raise coal prices. After a short time, he said, they will reduce the miners' weekly hours so, in the end, they will be no better off.

Unable to confirm that story, I did not report it. But the scenario played out almost precisely as predicted. My source, no wild-eyed radical, was A.C. Spurr, chairman of Monongahela Power and Light. The utility chief had little respect for the coal owners, union chiefs, or the coal-owning railroads. Instead of working against the public interest, he argued, they should be joining hands to develop economical ways to produce clean coal. Clean coal! That was over half a century ago.

What a missed opportunity. In the decades since, coal has earned such a negative reputation from air pollution, mine disasters, environmental abuse, and horrid mountaintop removal that the industry's current clean coal campaign tends to fall on deaf ears. The chance to make appropriate use of a storehouse of fuel that could serve the nation's crying need for energy for the next couple centuries may have been lost.

Old King Coal

Editor Smith invited me to try my hand at editorials for the *Fairmont Times*, so I wrote one complaining about coal trains being assembled in railyards adjacent to downtown Fairmont, raising clouds of dust and crashing all through the night. As Smith tore up my piece he said, "Enjoy that noise and breathe that coal dust, boy, they're the life blood of Appalachia." That attitude, by a local leader much admired for his civic spirit and intellect, is still common in the region. It lets absentee coal monopolists off the hook and helps explain why King Coal still reigns. Even when the rest of America prospers, depression persists in large sectors of the coal producing states and is likely to continue until the land rights message gains momentum.

NOTES

1. Hyslop's forecast about the future rise in the price of coal occurred before environmentalists began to argue for an end to dependence on fossil fuels. Yet coal remains the predominant source of electric power generation. Whether

its primacy as an energy source will persist for another century is difficult to predict.

2 Allegheny-Pittsburgh Coal Co. v County Comm'n, 488 US 336 (1989).

3 West Virginia properties were assessed for tax purposes at 50 percent of market value, so Morton actually valued the company's coal holdings at $12 million and then $15 million.

4 Robert Jerome Glennon, "Taxation and Equal Protection," in *George Washington University Law Review*, January 1990, recounts the government's comlicity with resource owners in denying the public its rights to some of nature's greatest gifts.

PART VII

RECLAIMING AMERICA

PUBLIC COLLECTION of land values to replace taxes that suppress the economy is a strategy that for too long has been missing in action from the American policy agenda. Without substantial taxation of socially created land values, many public and private remedies for treating social ills are rendered impotent.

Famous architect Frank Lloyd Wright agreed. "Why not make more free to 'the poor' the land they were born to inherit as they inherit the air to breathe and daylight to see by and water to drink? Henry George clearly enough showed us the simple basis of poverty in human society. Some organic solution of this land problem is not only needed, it is imperative."[1]

To get from here to there, Henry George offered the following advice: "Social reform is not to be secured by noise and shouting; by complaints and denunciation; by the formation of parties, or the making of revolutions; but by the awakening of thought and the progress of ideas. Until there be right thought, there cannot be right action; and when there is correct thought, right action will follow."

NOTE

1. Frank Lloyd Wright, *The Disappearing City,* FLW Collected Writings, Vol. 3, Rizzoli International, New York, 1932, reprinted 1993.

31

Ten Vital Paths

FOLLOWING ARE TEN MAJOR policy directions that can bolster America's economy. If followed, they can help make our nation once again a role model for people throughout the world who are struggling to overcome grinding poverty and exploitation.

1. Create Abundant Jobs at Living Wages

Substitute land taxes for taxes on wages and sales

Obviously, real wages are higher if fewer taxes are taken out of people's earnings, and wages retain more buying power if fewer taxes are imposed on people's spending.

Less obvious is that affordable land opens the door to jobs and businesses. Opportunities for employment and enterprises arise when people have places to function. When they can't afford land, their opportunities are constricted. Every official and designer of job creation programs should be cognizant of this critical fact: *idle lands equal idle hands.*

A beauty of land taxes is that they bring down the rents or prices people pay for work sites. Most taxes have the opposite effect, raising the prices of the things that are taxed. This counter-intuitive behavior of land taxes may be illustrated as follows:

A shopkeeper decides to buy a nearby parking lot he's been renting for $10,000 a year. The owner asks $200,000 – what he has to invest elsewhere, assuming a 5 percent interest rate, to get his same annual return ($200,000 x .05 = $10,000).

Imposing a 1 percent property tax of $2,000 on this reduces the owner's *net rent* to $8,000 a year. To maintain that yield if he sells, the owner drops his asking price to $160,000 ($8,000 divided by .05). If the tax is 2 percent, or $4,000, the net rent becomes $6,000 and the selling price is $120,000. *The higher the tax, the lower the selling price.*

Can't the owner sell the lot for $200,000 and let the buyer worry about the land tax? He would like to. But other land-holders, also faced with the higher tax, unload sites they have been keeping off the market. Competition from all sites being sold or rented checks the ability of any one owner to shift the tax cost to buyers. And the shopkeeper, aware of the $2,000 tax, would find $160,000, not $200.000, an acceptable price.

Officials and many economists insist employment is a "lagging indicator", that joblessness will persist until a depressed economy picks up. This is backward thinking. Jobs can and should be a *leading indicator.* If land prices are brought down to enable vigorous job creation, the resulting earnings of workers and enterprises will create an immediate demand for goods and services and get the wheels of production whirring.

2. Assure Affordable Housing for All

Stop taxing houses and apartments and tax the land *under* dwellings

America has *no housing problem.* This is no misprint, despite the story drummed into the public that the economic meltdown stemmed from *housing* prices which inflated until the bubble burst. Not so. Runaway *land* prices and mortgages based on them became chips in a gambling binge that led homeowners and the credit industry on a ride that was bound to crash.

Japan's earlier economic collapse should have forewarned us. Land values in the city of Tokyo escalated to such a frenzied point that they exceeded the land values of the entire United States before they brought Japan's economy to its knees.[1]

HERZL'S HOUSING VISION FOR ISRAEL

Half a century before Theodore Herzl's dream of a Jewish state would be realized, he was thinking ahead about how to provide housing. The following are telegram-like notes he wrote to himself:*

June 12, 1895. *Everyone, if possible, to attain a little house of his own. Rental and amortization for these houses. In the construction industry (whether for housing, railroads, highways, or the like) we will materially aid private enterprise by the grant of wholesale credits. The Society* [Herzl's proposed governing body] *will profit only through the increase of land values. Construction is to be cheap, because building enhances the value of the land.*

November 25, 1895. *I stand suddenly in another world... A good idea ... to levy a progressive tax on landed property. Henry George!*

One wonders, since fights over land and water rights are a big part of the ongoing Middle East struggles, if Herzl's vision had actually been applied, whether it would have enabled the Palestinians and Israelis to find a satisfactory way out of their conflict.

* Marvin Lowenthal, ed., translator, *The Diaries of Theodore Herzl*, Dial Press, New York, 1956.

An alleged housing crisis in the mid-1980s led me to analyze three and a half decades of data. I found that the labor, management, and building material costs affecting housing simply kept pace with inflation, rising about 200 percent over 35 years, closely tracking the Consumer Price Index. Residential *land* costs during the same period skyrocketed close to 2,000 percent! (See chart on page 194

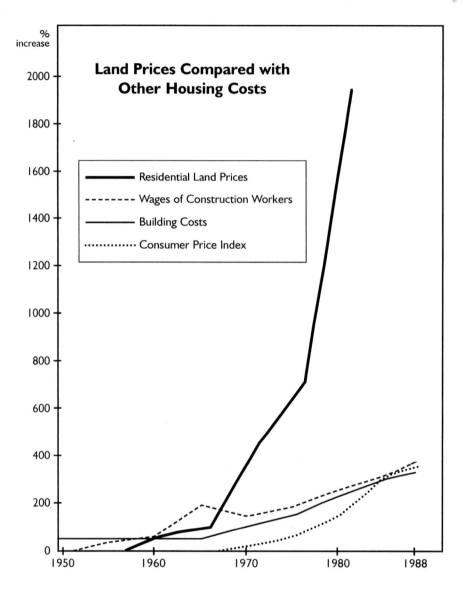

from *Affordable Housing: A Missing Link*, W. Rybeck, Center for Public Dialogue, Kensington, MD, 1988.)

The focus on affordable *housing* when the problem was affordable *land* led to fallacious policymaking. Rent subsidies, vouchers, rent controls, builder incentives, mortgage rate adjustments, and so forth, all related to housing, were tried. Some of these "solutions" exacerbated land price escalation, yet the behavior of the land market that lay at the core of the problem was totally ignored.

Substantial land taxes will hold land prices at realistic levels and keep housing costs within reach for almost everyone. Housing can then resume its proper and traditional role as *a place to live*, not as an investment or get-rich-quick machine. A mortgage can then resume its role as a means to spread out housing costs during a family's working years, not as a stake in a gambling spree.

3. Let Infrastructure Be Self-Financing

Governments should recapture the value that infrastructure creates

Repairing the nation's unsafe bridges, crumbling roads, bursting water mains, decrepit schools, and other failing facilities will cost an estimated $1.6 trillion.[2] To proceed with this, it is commonly assumed, will require deep deficits at a time when further deficits are taboo.

Here's good news for a change. The cost to the government could be minimal. Infrastructure creates its own *revolving fund* in the form of the land values it generates, and governments have the means to recoup these values.

The Metro subway system in the Washington, D.C. region is a case in point. As noted in Chapter 16, it spawned billions of dollars of new land values along its route, enough to cover its construction and operating costs.[3] Similarly, in New York City, the Verrazano Narrows Bridge caused land values on the Staten Island side alone to increase by double the bridge's cost.[4]

Unfortunately, the revolving funds are not revolving. If a worker turned down his paycheck while his family went hungry, he would be considered soft in the head. Yet governments act this way, failing to pick up their legitimate earnings and letting owners of lands adjacent to public works pocket the bulk of these values. Private gain from public investments is an old story in America. But that is no reason for perpetuating this practice. An enlightened value-capture policy will enable the nation to wipe out its infrastructure backlog.

4. Stop Sprawl and Urban Decay

Resolve these interrelated problems in one blow by taxing land values

Sick cities and sprawl are opposite sides of the same coin. People and businesses fleeing cities invade surrounding farms, forests, and scenic areas. To halt this exodus and protect the environment depends on making urban areas more appealing and more affordable. This cannot happen when significant portions of cities' desirable sites are over-priced and kept in cold storage by land speculation, forcing people and firms to move out in search of cheaper land.

Some development interests advertise this sprawl as the flowering of the American Dream. It has become an American Nightmare. Scattershot growth patterns waste farmland and energy, magnify traffic congestion, and boost taxes to pay for duplicating public works.

Blight and crime give cities a bad name. Media exaggeration of these defects can make people forget the positive qualities of cities. At their best, towns and cities are seedbeds of culture, science, and the arts. They foster face-to-face relationships that generate cooperation, neighborliness, and mutual trust. They facilitate commerce and production. Giving up on cities would be a grave mistake.

Land speculation erodes many plans and efforts to reinvigorate cities. This speculation takes various forms – slums, porn strips, surface parking lots, derelict boarded-up stores and apartments, and empty lots. Their owners invest little, waiting to cash in after public agencies and productive neighbors make these properties worth more.

Firms that would prefer to locate in town become refugees of a sort, driven to search for affordable suburban or exurban sites. There they confront further speculators who block compact growth and force development to scatter inefficiently across the landscape. Land speculation is rampant, not because of evil people, but because an incoherent tax system makes it remunerative. Communities can take the profit out of it. Replacing taxes on enterprise with robust taxes on land gives land speculators a gentle push into productive activities. This encourages infill growth in towns and cities and relieves the pressure on developers to invade farmland and scenic areas.

5. Rationalize the Nation's Tax System

Substitute beneficial land taxes for injurious taxes through five bargains

All taxes are not created equal. A mistaken view that all taxes are detrimental, necessary evils at best, has gained currency. Public finance professionals, seeking to minimize the harm from any one tax, promote a "balanced" tax approach with a mix of taxes for cities and states.[5] This is like trying to reduce the danger of a car's poor steering by "balancing" it with a bad engine, bad tires, and bad brakes. Bargains therefore need to be struck to elevate constructive and beneficial taxes and to phase out detrimental ones.

Bargain #1 – **Abolish most exemptions, deductions, credits and other IRS loopholes in exchange for greatly reduced personal income tax rates.** An early appeal of the "progressive" income tax was the Robin Hood principle, taking from the wealthy to aid the poor. Voters and legislators failed to foresee that high-powered lawyers and lobbyists would fashion endless ways to shelter incomes of the rich and shift tax burdens back to poorer people. A tax code that spawns a huge industry dedicated to disguising the earnings of the affluent is clearly out of control. Big tax rate reductions would increase compliance and minimize the billions now lost from both illegal tax evasion and more or less legal tax avoidance.

Bargain #2 – **Greatly reduce taxes on business profits in exchange for taxes on the unimproved value of locations and raw materials used by businesses.** It is hard to justify funding government by seizing sizeable shares of the profits of production when that slows down the economy. It is hard *not* to justify governments' right to recoup values created by *nature* and *society*. Businesses should welcome a chance to keep their gains from enterprise in exchange for reimbursing governments for all the amenities that give value to their lands – nature's raw materials, advantageous locations, and all the public facilities and services they enjoy.

Bargain #3 – **Abolish property taxes on improvements in exchange for taxes on socially created site values.** Unpopularity of the property tax stems largely from the part that penalizes people for improving homes and other structures. Many states and localities abolished the *personal* property tax imposed on furnishings, inventories, and machinery.[6] The next logical step is to remove the tax on improvements that discourages care of the built environment. The property tax will then be a pure land tax that embraces all of its constructive features.

Assessments form the foundation of property tax administration.[7] Enlightened localities assess all parcels reliably and fairly. They assess land and buildings separately. They value land according to what buyers are currently paying for sites, not according to the use or non-use of the sites. They re-assess annually or every few years to account for market changes. They maintain open books so neighbors can easily check if they are being treated uniformly. They provide easy appeals machinery for correcting errors and keeping assessors on their toes. And they state valuations at 100 percent of market value, avoiding fractional assessments that hide errors, confuse taxpayers, and camouflage favoritism.

Bargain #4 – **Greatly reduce sales and excise taxes in exchange for setting public domain leases for mineral extraction, grazing rights, and so forth at current market values.** Value added taxes, favored by many income tax opponents, are a variety of sales tax. The difference between taxes on sales and earnings is largely a matter of timing. A payroll tax reduces people's wages before they get them; sales taxes shrink wages after they are in people's pockets. It is widely recognized that sales taxes hit lower income people hardest. The dampening effect of sales taxes is readily illustrated by sales tax holidays that unleash buying binges.

The federal government should make it a priority to correct the scandalously low rents for leasing grazing, timber, and mining rights on public lands. Auctions and frequent re-evaluations would halt a continuous raid on our national treasures. The government should also halt the giveaway of the public's airwaves and internet spectrum. Leasing this common property would produce revenue, strike a blow against special privilege, and revive media competition.

BROADCAST SPECTRUM – PRIVATE OR COMMON PROPERTY?

The late William Safire got it right when he wrote, "In terms of ripping off the taxpayers with not a peep from the media, nothing compares with the broadcasters' lobby. This phalanx of freeloaders has stolen the free use of great chunks of the most valuable natural resource of the information age: the digital television spectrum owned by the American people."* NBC, ABC and CBS won Safire's ire because, when their old gift of the analog spectrum was being superseded by the digital bandwidth, they demanded and won a gift of that too. "When a few of us suggested that this national resource be opened to competitive bidding rather than given away, the broadcasters insisted that the airwaves were their entitlement," he said. This "foolish and craven" giveaway by a Republican Congress and the Clinton White House to broadcasters is now worth many times the original $70 billion cost to taxpayers.

* *New York Times*, October 9, 2000.

Bargain #5 – **Abolish taxes on savings in exchange for eliminating preferential tax treatment of land value gains.** Encouraging savings by freeing them from taxation would help counteract Americans' growing tendency to dangerously overload themselves with debt. A sensible revenue alternative is to tax the gains in land value that are incorrectly termed "capital gains". A low tax on capital gains is presumed to induce the creation of more capital. No amount of tax favoritism will add to the supply of land. In fact, encouraging investment in land will divert economic actors from the producing of goods and services to the destructive betting on land values.

In sum, one might think it is self-evident that an enterprise system should avoid taxes that suppress enterprise. However, since such taxes are used by federal, state, and local governments, it needs to be underscored that a pro-enterprise alternative is to rely primarily on taxing the value of land and raw resources, plus user fees.[8] Because land is out in the open, not readily hidden, billions in revenue will not be lost from an underground economy or other forms of tax evasion. The conditions that formerly undergirded America's dynamic economy – cheap land, minimal taxation of producers, and genuine competition – can be brought back to life with these reforms.

6. Maximize Public Transportation

Public transit should be safe, cheap, convenient, and comfortable

For inter-city transportation, America needs to restore and modernize its railroads. Funds for a world-class rail system can be offset to a significant degree by reducing the incidence and costs of congestion, auto accidents, and highway widenings. The chances to achieve major energy savings alone should dictate prompt action on this front.

To reduce the squandered hours and stress from gridlock, urban areas should make mass transit a top priority. Fares should be low to maximize transit use. Services should be provided mainly for the compactly developed parts of a metropolis. Extending bus or train routes to far-flung parts of a metropolis tends to give developers a green light to create more sprawl.

What if businesses absorbed the full costs of a form of urban transportation that brings people to their precincts? *They actually do this*. They offer a system for moving people that is free and on call within moments. This is *vertical* transportation. Elevators and escalators! No building or store owner would think of charging passengers for this service. High-rise properties would be worth little above the third floor if employees, customers, and tenants could not use this service to freely go up and down at will. Transit planners and merchants should take notice. If firms agree it is good business to give customers a free ride to the seventh floor, is it not equally good business to subsidize *horizontal* transportation to bring customers seven miles to use their shops, cafes, or doctors' offices?

7. Equalize Educational Opportunities

Shift school funding to states to treat kids in rich and poor districts equitably

Widely disparate levels of per-pupil spending from one school district to another violate the promised guarantees of equal educational opportunity in most state constitutions. Courts in the 1970s found that reliance on *local* property taxes for school funding was unacceptable because it short-changed students in districts with low property values. However, the courts did not close the door to *statewide* property taxation or, better yet, statewide land value taxation. With the latter, states can distribute funds from the common wealth of the entire state according to formulas based on numbers of pupils and other demographics. Control of school administration can continue at the local level.

Equal spending is no guarantee of equal quality. But quality schooling is difficult to attain if funding for first-rate teachers is grossly inadequate. A high floor of funding should be set for all students in a state. Then, if a district wants to tax itself more heavily to provide a quality higher than the norm, they need not be precluded from doing so.

The anti-sprawl effect of state land taxes will spare schools from two costly matters. One is the present need to build new schools in outlying areas when inner-city schools close for lack of pupils. Another is the maintaining of large fleets of school buses to serve ever longer routes. Another virtue of statewide school funding is that it will relieve cities and counties from what is often their largest budget item, enabling them to more easily afford their other obligations.

8. Stop Tax Evaders from Moving Capital Offshore

Restore America as the world's premier business location

To escape U.S. taxes, too many home-grown corporations move their headquarters to the Caribbean. Many wealthy citizens stash their fortunes in overseas accounts. Calls for severely penalizing them reflect the anger of citizens who are taxed more heavily because tax evaders fail to pay their share. Yet, so long as taxpayers and businesses feel our tax system is confiscatory and unfair, halting this flight to tax havens is like trying to force water to flow uphill.

Companies and savings can be brought back from foreign shores by restoring integrity and justice into our tax system. Corporations will no longer flee when their best chance to thrive is right here. Nor will private money flee when savings and investments produce higher after-tax interest at home than elsewhere. If the words "tax haven" did not have such a negative connotation, one would be tempted to say that our national goal should be to "Make the U.S.A. the premier tax haven" with user-friendly taxes for people and for businesses.

9. Empower State and Local Governments

Reform revenue systems so cities and states can control their own destinies

Close-to-the-people governments can be a reality, not a distant memory of an era when independent localities were breeding grounds of innovation, training grounds for political leaders, and binders of personal relationships that built trust and integrity in business and social circles.

New York City some decades ago cried "Uncle" – meaning Uncle Sam – when it faced bankruptcy. The Big Apple pleaded poverty while it sat on the nation's richest lode of urban land values. The city only lightly tapped that lode created by its own public works and by its millions of people vying for space. Instead, it relied on taxpayers elsewhere to bail it out.

In 2009 California suffered more than most states from the national fiscal collapse, in no small part because it had wrecked its property tax by enacting the infamous Proposition 13.[9]

Governors and mayors can revive their economies without repeatedly going hat in hand to Washington. They can tax their abundant land values, their greatest resource. This will free them from the federal rules and controls that are the price for accepting most federal loans and grants.

10. Foster a Sustainable Economy

Eliminate barriers to healthy commerce, industry, and farming

Some have given up on America's ability to restore its industrial might, reinvigorate large and small businesses, or reverse the decline of family farms. Such pessimism is not warranted. These goals can be attained if we stop neglecting a prime factor in all production, the land. Noted briefly are examples of how land policy changes can substantially improve the economic landscape.

- Corporations often act against their own long-term interests in pursuit of tax advantages. Greatly reducing taxes on their profits means they will no longer shoot for short-term gains from strategies that are economically unsound. Taxing them instead on the land value of their real estate simply induces them to make optimal use of their landholdings and to get on with their basic production mission.
- Start-up businesses are hindered by high land costs. Land-based taxes not only reduce these costs but also open up for entrepreneurs many ideal locations that have been held off the market by speculators.
- Start-up farms are also hindered by high land costs. Real farmers are blocked out by absentee owners who are "farming" land values instead of crops. A robust land tax puts genuine farmers back in the driver's seat, or tractor's seat. Moreover, land taxation can open the quantities of lands well suited for agriculture that are now held fallow. This will avert farming in inappropriate arid areas requiring huge quantities of water for irrigation, or in denuded rain forests.
- Consolidations increasingly sap the vitality of the economy. Heavily taxing the value of natural resources makes it costlier to hoard and monopolize them. Freeing up these resources increases opportunities for competition.
- The economy is undercut by pursuit of land value gains – what economists aptly call *unearned income*. The time and energy devoted to this activity produce no land; in fact, they produce nothing, but they do impede job and commercial growth. Letting the public capture land value gains leaves to private

individuals and firms the pursuit of gains from their creation
of goods and services. This is the reverse of current laws that
make anti-productive land speculation more profitable than
genuine production.

- Another diversion from a wholesome economy is a dispropor-
tionate attention to manipulating the supply of money and
credit, plus exotic forms of IOUs and hedges. Of course
government should use its power to assure the soundness of
financial instruments because they lubricate the economy.
However, money and credit are not wealth – we cannot eat
them, drive them, or live in them. They facilitate trade, but
that presupposes the existence of things to trade. An emphasis
on basic land policies to create a favorable business climate will
enable job creation and businesses and factories to be left
largely alone so they may "come back home" like Little Bo
Peep's sheep.

- Strong public reaction against urban decay, demolition of
architectural treasures, and a throwaway-cities mentality gave
birth to a potent historic preservation movement. The buildings being saved represent only a partial victory when they are
surrounded by a sea of blight. To complete the victory requires
restoration of the *historic economic environment* that saw our
cities thrive – an environment of high land taxes that fostered
vibrant downtowns and attractive neighborhoods. Architect
Hans Blumenthal saw this need when he wrote: "There is no
doubt that the present real property tax ... contributes more
to depressing the standard of housing than all government
housing policies combined do to raise it."[10] A classic instance
of current property tax disincentives involved the stunningly
beautiful 38-story Seagram Building erected in New York City
half a century ago. Instead of assessing it at its $17 million
market value, the tax commission, upheld by the courts,
assessed it at $26 million because of its beauty and "prestige
value", as the court put it. An editorial in *Life* magazine called
this a "tax formula to make certain that American cities stay
ugly and get uglier".[11]

- Population and immigration pressures are often cited as
obstacles to economic upturns. The common belief that there
is a direct correlation between high population density and
poverty does not hold up. Think of the Netherlands with 1,034

prosperous people per square mile and Albania with 286 pitifully poor people per square mile. Comparisons showing the opposite can also be drawn. Thus what seems likely is that *population is a magnifier.* That is, population intensifies existing social conditions, good or bad. Crowd more people into places where exploitation and misery predominate and the situation will worsen. But add more people in places where equity and well-being flourish and they will boost the level of prosperity. To the extent this is so, it strengthens the argument for taking steps to assure a just and harmonious relationship between people and the land. Then the earth's cornucopia of resources and civilization's productive genius should combine to wipe out much of the poverty in the nation and in the world.

NOTES

1. "Tokyo's real estate, once collateralized at the going rate of 80 percent of its market value, would be worth $8 trillion – enough to buy *all* United States real estate and *all* U.S. companies on the stock exchanges." Kenichi Ohmae, *Washington Post*, January 15, 1989. Also, "At $15 trillion, the 1988 market value of land in Japan was five times that in the U.S." Marcus W. Brauchli and Masayoshi Kanabayashi, *Wall Street Journal*, March 23, 1989. Land speculation became so all-consuming that the Japanese turned to spending billions in buying prime United States real estate such as the Rockefeller Center.
2. The American Society of Civil Engineers, after an inventory of the nation's infrastructure repair needs, reported in July 2007 that meeting the total cost would require expenditures of $320 billion a year for five years.
3. W. Rybeck, "Metrorail Impacts on Washington Area Land Values," House Committee on Banking, Finance and Urban Affairs, January 1981.
4. A New York Plan Association study reported that increased accessibility of their sites gave Staten Island landowners a $700 million windfall from the span which, at a cost of $350 million, linked their island to Brooklyn.
5. *Principles of a High Quality State Revenue System*, National Conference of State Legislatures, John Shannon, Robert Klein, Steven D. Gold, 1st edition, 1992, updated 2007. The stated principles of a good tax system are exemplary, yet the specific taxes recommended fail to meet these criteria. Pertinent quotes: "All taxes have advantages and disadvantages, but reliance on a diverse assortment can cancel out their biases." Relying on numerous revenue sources can "keep rates low to minimize the impact on behavior" of any one harmful tax and "... avoid excessive reliance on any single revenue system."

6. The personal property tax became known as "a tax on honesty" because only the most conscientious and naïve individuals and firms revealed a full accounting of their assets or paid what the law required.
7. The late John Callaway, a Chicago broadcaster, pundit, and homespun philosopher, wrote: "Isn't it true that any system as inherently, deliberately complicated as the property tax assessment system ought to be scrapped?" *The Thing of It Is*, Jameson Books, 1994, Ottawa, IL. Too many states and localities, unfortunately, deserved this criticism.
8. User charges help conserve scarce resources like water that are squandered unless they are priced high enough to restrain waste. In the case of specialized services like public golf courses, user charges target players rather than non-players to support the facility.
9. In late 2009 Frank Walker, an attorney in Chula Vista, formed Prosper California, an organization that planned to launch an initiative calling for a complete overhaul of California's tax system, substituting land taxes for taxes that discourage productive activities. In short, it is a proposal designed along lines recommended in this book.
10. *Metropolis and Beyond*, Wiley, New York, 1979.
11. August 16, 1963.

32

Recovery, Jobs
and Social Harmony

IDEOLOGICAL RIFTS plague our legislative machinery and society at large. A just land policy has the potential to bridge these divisions because of its appeal to people of diverse philosophic leanings. It speaks to the many concerns of different groups.

- A land tax regimen strengthens the market system, ends excessive taxation of production, and limits government's role in the economy – results that echo cardinal issues voiced by conservatives.
- A land tax regimen minimizes special privileges, ends excessive taxes on wages, and calls for a firmer public role in guaranteeing equal opportunity for all – central results called for by liberals.
- Shifting taxes off production on to land values will result in full employment, healthier cities, a greener countryside, and elimination of a major cause of economic collapses – results yearned for by people of all political stripes.

The unifying effect of these social justice ideals is already foreseen in their advocacy by scientists and theologians, labor and business leaders, conservatives, liberals, and centrists. Rarely does one find a William F. Buckley, Jr, a Martin Luther King, Jr, a Winston Churchill, and an Albert Einstein all praising the same reform. All are on record as strongly favoring land value taxation. This approach to social equity and progress has for too long been suppressed. Never timelier, it addresses victims of the last bust as well as those who want to prevent another binge of land speculation before it spirals out of control.

The Promise of Systemic Reform

Measures citied in preceding chapters offer hope of fostering a stable and steady prosperity. They are designed to enable all the people – everyone able and willing to work – to participate in economic progress. Experience has shown that these measures lead to more plentiful jobs, more new and thriving businesses, more competition in the extraction of natural resources, and more affordable housing. Reliance on revenue sources that stimulate rather than depress the economy will, by greatly reducing the need for subsidies and welfare expenditures, help free America from its crushing national debt levels.

Skepticism about the potency of the land policy changes is understandable. The role of land has been AWOL, absent without leave, from the public dialogue for several generations.

The burden of proof, however, falls on those who favor the current tax system and associated policies. These have failed to generate a sustainable prosperity. They led to the gaping gap between the super-rich and the super-poor. They oversaw the decline in American production of consumer goods and heavy industry. They led to the deterioration of public amenities in cities and towns. It is against this state of affairs that any alternative approach must be measured.

Our present economic policies constitute a ticking time bomb as threatening to America as any external menace. It is tempting to think that tinkering with tighter regulations will keep "excessive exuberance" in check, but analysis suggests they will not suffice in the absence of systemic reforms.

A just social order cannot co-exist with an unjust tax system. People on the middle and lower rungs of the income ladder may not understand how they are being exploited. If told that their hardships stem from denial of their land rights, most would have no notion of what that means. Yet their dissatisfaction, frustration, and sometimes their violent lashing out are signs that America is in deeper trouble than we like to admit.

Preventing boom-and-bust cycles is a moral no less than an

economic issue. If a privileged class is getting something for nothing – enriching itself while producing nothing of value – then the underprivileged are to that extent being deprived of the fruits of their labor. As if this were not unfair enough, governments come along and, kicking someone who is already down, further diminish people's rightful earnings.

Overturning the inequitable and injurious treatment of common property will restore the proper treatment of and respect for private property. By so doing, we can usher in a new burst of freedom, a new era of prosperity that extends to all members of society, and a revived sense of trust in our democratic institutions. This will enable our country once more to be a light and a trailblazer among the community of nations. We can do it. It is time to reclaim America.

APPENDIX A

Education Alone
Could Fail

FOLLOWING are excerpts from an article with the above title by W. Rybeck that appeared in *Antioch Notes*, Vol. 41, No. 6, published in Yellow Springs, Ohio, March 1964, in response to the main thrust of the newly-declared War on Poverty.

Education is suddenly grasped as the magic key to unlock the jobs that 5 percent of Americans are unable to find.

Those who glibly say education will cure our high rate of joblessness might well recall the 1930s. Then PhD's by the score studied bread lines. Nobody suggests that hundreds of thousands of educated Americans somehow became uneducated and unfit to hold jobs. If college graduates happened to be Negro, it was not for lack of education that these scholars went begging for employment as day laborers or railroad porters.

Factories, businesses, and service institutions discovered during World War II that they could fit the most unlikely prospects – from the standpoint of schooling or experience – into semi-skilled and often skilled occupations. Training was accomplished on the job and with amazing speed. Wartime pressures and patriotism helped, but cold-cash incentives, spurring industry to produce at full steam, made management happy for the chance to hire any Rosie and train her as a riveter.

Planning an entire work force that is above average has a nice democratic ring to it – but it is mathematically impossible.

Education's most potent contribution today would be not mere schooling, but throwing light on the causes and cures of shrinking job opportunity.

We might hint that the jungle of special privileges incorporated into our society would be a likely place to stalk some of these causes. We might note further that tracks leading into economic quagmires suggest that growing concentrations of corporate power, job restrictions by unions, and urban land tenure inequities are extremely ripe for penetrating studies. Surely exploitation and monopoly, for instance, will not vanish from feeding better educated victims to these job-destroying dragons.

Education can be sold on the basis of its own enduring values, not as a too easily punctured ballooning hope for bringing millions of new jobs into being.

APPENDIX B

Many Voices on Land Policy Reform Issues

FOLLOWING are brief excerpts from "HUD and the Property Tax", a collection of articles, letters and Congressional testimony presented by the author to the Department of Housing and Urban Development and to the White House. Although the views represented a distinct contrast to majority economic thinking at the time, they showed that a potent minority of thoughtful people were linking land and land tax issues to urban and economic woes in the 1950s and 1960s. Writers are identified by their positions at the time. The author's suggested federal actions to promote property tax modernization, offered in the presentation, conclude this appendix.

E.V. and E.G. Rostow, political science professors (in *The Urban Condition*, by L.J. Duhl): The [conventional] property tax ... is one of the most influential breeders of waste in the economy, including the movement of business and of people from the cities to suburbs which involve the premature abandonment and destruction of huge capital resources in the roads, sewers, gas mains, fire stations, houses, schools and electrical equipment of existing urban areas – investments which then have to be duplicated in the suburbs. The social and political consequences ... are even more serious than the economic wastefulness.

Congressman Thomas W. Curtis (R-Missouri): [T]he development of a modernized real estate property tax is the basic land reform needed by almost all the so-called economically underdeveloped countries. A well-designed real estate tax is a discouragement to the greatest of all economic sins – to hoard rather than to utilize wealth.

Grady Clay, Editor, *Landscape Architecture Journal* (in memo to author, 9/16/1966): It is vital that a fair and equitable method be worked out to return to the public purse a larger share of the "windfall profits" in unearned land values. I therefore recommend that legislation should be prepared for introduction into Congress which will require – as a condition of all federal grants – that local property tax procedures be improved so as to speed up the application of increased property assessments on lands benefitted by Federal facilities. This requirement should be extended to land areas benefitted by Federally-funded highway construction; by Federal flood control and multi-purpose water development projects; by Federal open space and landscape grant programs; and by Federally-assisted urban renewal programs.

Lyle C. Bryant, economics professor, federal government economist and prime mover of the Rosslyn, Virginia property tax reform: Urban renewalists can expect to be a pretty frustrated lot until they grasp the point that through ill-conceived and poorly administered property taxes, which provide *perverse* incentives to private enterprise, most American cities are continuously creating the problems that the urban renewalists are devoting their lives to solving.

Dick Netzer, in *The Economics of the Property Tax* (Brookings, 1966): [I]t is difficult to find any flaws in the argument that the tax change [heavier taxation of site values combined with lower taxation of improvements] will tend to have favorable resource allocational effects.

Paul Ylvisaker, Director, Public Affairs Program, the Ford Foundation: Tax incentives ... go to the jugular vein of private decisions and have the combined effect of both carrot and stick. Both the local property tax and the federal income tax can be adapted so as to reward the man who maintains his property rather than the slumlord who exploits it and the slothful owner who lets it go... Stiff taxes might be imposed on those who pollute air, land or water.

Harlan Trott, Pacific News Bureau Chief, *Christian Science Monitor* **(letter to author, 9/19/66):** The way to rebuild our cities is a) stop federal windfall financing, and b) reinstate federal land taxes such as were used during the first hundred years of the Republic (*Financial History of America*, Davis Rich Dewey).

Richard W. Lindholm, Dean, School of Business Administration, University of Oregon, from paper given at 41st annual conference, Western Economic Association: The introduction of a state land value tax to support public education would permit all local governments to sharply cut ad valorem property tax rates on buildings and personal property.... The increase in the portion of property taxes resting on land values and the administration of the tax on a state-wide basis at a uniform rate would definitely place the property tax on the side of metropolitan unity instead of disunity as is now the case.

Max S. Wehrly, Director, Urban Land Institute, reported in *Dayton Daily News,* **9/25/65:** In Boston, buildings were taxed so heavily that the wealthiest entrepreneurs could not take part in urban renewal without special tax exemptions. The system's a mess. The ad valorem tax today puts a premium on neglect across the board.

Edwin P. Neilan, President, Bank of Delaware, Past President, U.S. Chamber of Commerce (letter to author 9/13/66): The Federal Government might well write some standards for land or site value taxation as one of the prerequisites for urban renewal projects.

Mason Gaffney, Chair, Economics Department, University of Wisconsin-Milwaukee, in "Property Taxes and the Frequency of Urban Renewal," National Tax Association: If they [land taxes] simply raise revenue without doing much damage, they are a great improvement over what we have now... It lets us escape from the folly of taxing improvements.

Robert F. Steadman, Director, Committee for Economic Development (letter to author, 9/2/66): Our recent policy statement noted that real property assessments in most parts of the country "may be accurately described as inequitable, inefficient, incompetent, or corrupt." If local governments cannot even administer their primary revenue source more fairly, in accordance with law, what major responsibility can we expect them to perform effectively?

Robert M. Hutchins, President, Center for the Study of Democratic Institutions, in "Our Ramshackle Tax Structure", *Los Angeles Times*. 1/11/64: The tax system almost compels the buyer of land to become a speculator. If he improves his land, his property tax will rise. If, on the other hand, he sits on the land, does nothing with it and sells at a great profit, he will pay little by way of property tax and will be taxed on the profit at favorable rates applied to capital gains.

Bill Burns, Editor, *San Diego Labor Leader*, "Land Speculation Major Source of Evil", 8/22/63: As long as slums remain that profitable, they will continue to grow despite subsidized urban renewal programs – unless something also is done about increasing land taxes and reducing taxes on improvements. Such an approach... would take the profit out of slums and provide a powerful lever on owners of blighted areas to tear them down and build anew.

John R. Fuchs, Judge, 22nd Judicial District, New Bramfels, Texas, in *Land and Liberty*, London, July 1958: What is this thing, this value, this fund or intangible asset that is created by the people and by the government which belongs to all the people? Is it not the annual value of land – ground rent – or the "economic rent" as the economist calls it? ... [T]here is still one basic God-given right which we have not fully recognized. It is the right of the people to the use of a part of the earth given to them – the children of man – from which and by which alone they can live.

A Tentative Strategy for HUD

1. Assist in upgrading the professionalism of state and local property tax officials.
2. Let local property tax modernization be a condition for obtaining federal grants.
3. Offer to hold states and localities harmless from fiscal loss when they shift property taxes off buildings on to land values (even though such loss is unlikely).

4. Promote research on impacts of both the conventional and two-rate property tax.
5. Halt federal tax policies – depreciation allowances, capital gains favoritism applied to land value gains, and certain deductibles – that encourage land speculation.
6. Reinstate federal land taxes to recapture values created by federally-funded infrastructure.
7. Make property tax modernization a major feature of foreign assistance programs.
8. Coordinate land use and land tax policies with other agencies – Defense, Agriculture, Commerce, Interior, Transportation and so forth.

APPENDIX C

Douglas Commission Testimony

TRANSCRIPTIONS OF HEARINGS held in 18 cities across the nation were printed in *Hearings before the National Commission on Urban Problems* (Vols. 1-5, Government Printing Office, 1968, Library of Congress No. 68-60024). The publication is a goldmine of information about a range of that era's urban problems, many of which still persist. A minute sample of testimony pertinent to the subject of this book follows.

James W. Rouse, developer of the new town of Columbia, Maryland: When Pittsburgh did the Golden Triangle, it was the first time anybody had really gone in and done anything about the ragged edge of any downtown area. From all over the country people have come to Pittsburgh to see the Golden Triangle. And this really became the father of commercial redevelopment. It worked.

Joseph M. Barr, Mayor of Pittsburgh: Gateway Center at the base of the Golden Triangle was financed privately in its entirety, except for the construction of publicly-owned streets and property... [Taxing] land at double the rate of buildings has generally helped to encourage the improvement of real estate, especially the building of large commercial buildings. I also believe the system has been particularly fair and beneficial to homeowners.

Rev. Sidney Daniels, President, Harlem Park Neighborhood Council, Baltimore: The tax base on slum housing is so low that it makes slum housing extremely profitable. Many landlords, therefore, avoid their responsibility in the proper maintenance of housing. Deterioration is thus caused by inadequate maintenance, decreasing the annual tax. The fact of less taxes makes the property more profitable to rent.

Howard Offit, President, R.S. Construction Co., and President, Property Owners Association of Baltimore: I would like to recommend some consideration to the [high] tax assessment of residential property owners who spend sizeable sums of money on rehabilitation. Some moratorium might be given these owners as an incentive to do a good job or as a reward for their contribution to the community.

Juanita Mitchell, President, Maryland NAACP: If you cut down the tree of blight and leave the roots, no matter how many millions of tax funds you spend in building and improving the physical accommodations, you are going to have the burgeoning of the old tree of blight – the same situation that you spent millions to eliminate.

Hortense Gabel, New York City housing official: There are many major [slum] problems we have only recently begun to identify. These are the high cost of land and buildings; the high cost of money; the lack of development funds to cover preliminary legal, technical and acquisition costs; antiquated technology; and the failure to understand the links between standard dwellings and education, jobs, transportation, sanitation and other required services… We need to give some hard thinking to finding the incentives that will bring new forms of private investment to new and rehabilitated housing.

Richard L. Steiner, Director, Baltimore Urban Renewal and Housing Agency and Special Consultant to the secretary of HUD: I am increasingly convinced that much can and should be done to facilitate residential rehabilitation through modifications in taxation, both locally and nationally. Some property owners have been faced with increased real estate assessments as the reward for their cooperation with rehabilitation efforts. This sort of penalty for cooperation should be ended.

Richard E. Lee, Mayor of New Haven: [T]oo many cities are confined in their income from their tax base by the antiquated property tax, which is regressive and restrictive, and cannot be expanded to meet the expanding needs of the city and its people.

Jack Meltzer, Director, Center for Urban Studies, University of Chicago: The inability of the current urban renewal practices ... to guide and influence the character of non-acquired clearance and conservation areas results in a distortion of the public goals that motivated substantial public expenditures. The reliance on city zoning and housing and building codes to deal with these segments has largely proven ineffective. One possible corrective is the use of benefit assessments in renewal areas, as obtains in Britain, in which accretions in land values resulting from public programs are retained by the public or distributed to those who are disadvantageously affected by the public programs. This would also suggest examination of the land tax and of differential taxation.

Mitchell Sviridoff, Vice President, National Affairs, The Ford Foundation: As to resources, we are close to making a mockery of our lofty goals. New York City's guideline for community action programs this year is $17 million. With an estimated two million people in the city living in poverty, this means eight dollars and a few cents per person. To make a comparison [with the Depression of the 1930s] I quote Prof. Howard Zinn: "The poverty program draws on one-fifth of one percent of the gross national product. In 1938, FDR was spending fifteen times this percentage on public works alone, and that was not enough."

Columbus Kiensler, New Haven citizen: I heard Mayor Lee talking about housing projects. Where? I haven't seen them. He talked about tearing down old places. What do you have there now [where approximately 5,000 people lived]? You've got a hospital and a throughway. He's pushing us completely out, and in a way that he don't know – or maybe he know how he's doing it but he thinks other people can't even see it. Why don't you give me a decent place to live? I'm not asking for a million dollars. Mayor Lee is saying, "Build, build, build." What is he building? Parking lots. Ride through the city. You will see more parking lots than apartment houses.

Lawrence M. Cox, Executive Director, Norfolk (Virginia) Redevelopment and Housing Authority; President, American Society of

Planning Officials: Speculation [from urban renewal owned sites] could be avoided, and it should be avoided, by providing that any excess realized from the ultimate sale or lease of the land beyond the original investment, plus a reasonable interest or carrying charge, would be returned to the federal and local government on a two-thirds, one-third basis.

Lawrence DeNardis, Political Science Professor, Albertus Magnus College, speaking for the Ripon Society: A major barrier to adequate housing in the United States exists because of the property tax. As long as cities are compelled to rely on the [conventional] real estate tax that they can collect within their own confines, they are going to be encouraged, if not compelled, to seek industry and other heavy users of land that will pay high taxes in order to support schools and community services. Therefore, the pressure to increase the yield from real estate taxes compels cities to get out of the housing market and into the industrial-commercial one. And if they must "house", it is certainly not low-cost housing.

Edward J. Logue, Boston Development Administrator: If you look at what happens to a slumlord on the South Side of Chicago or in Harlem today, that slumlord can have a hundred violations on his property; he may not have put a dime into maintenance; but every year he can deduct depreciation. The Internal Revenue Code is helping him... The most effective way to collect revenue is through the federal income tax; the least effective way is to assess property here. The mayor of Boston has got to be very careful how much he tries to get out of real estate because the investment is mobile. The governor of Massachusetts has to be very careful because the governor of Arkansas keeps sending that [promotional] literature up here.

Barnet Lieberman, Executive Vice President, Philadelphia Housing Development Corporation: At the present time, at least in Philadelphia, our public assistance grants for shelter are subsidizing slumlords... Why do you have to build high-rise apartments [for public housing] in Philadelphia? It is because the cost of land is so high now. Philadelphia is a city of row houses, of homes.

George Romanos, Boston realtor (responding to a question about whether he had described himself as "the biggest slumlord in town"):

I have been described that way, so I accept it... It seems to be the policy that nonprofit groups should be designated as developers versus private enterprise, even though I have yet to find where nonprofit groups can even come anywhere near competing. Their construction cost is certainly about 40 percent more.

Mason Gaffney, Economics Professor, University of Wisconsin-Milwaukee: You can tax the very all out of a piece of land and it will never get up and walk out of town... The [conventional] property tax is calculated to inhibit, penalize and discourage whatever is new.

Arch M. Woodruff, Chancellor, University of Hartford: Where experience with this tax [a property tax based on site value only] has been substantial, the public accepts it.

Commission Chairman Paul H. Douglas: *Does not the owner of land appropriate the values we have created by expansion of population, labor and capital? (Answer)* **Jerome Rothenberg, Economics Professor, Massachusetts Institute of Technology:** That is what I am emphasizing and suggesting. **Douglas:** *You were all trying to avoid saying you believe in taxing the increase in rental land values. I believed it for 40 or 50 years. If I am wrong I would like to be set right. (Answer)* **Seymour Buskin, Law Firm Partner, Real Estate and Mortgage Counsel to Western Pennsylvania National Bank:** I think ultimately, land is a public ownership interest. **Douglas:** *I am not ready to go as far as that. I am a moderate. I would simply say the community is entitled to get a very large portion of this increase in land values.*

Raymond L. Richman, Professor of Economics and Social Development, University of Pittsburgh: Few if any economists challenge the conclusion that land taxation discourages the holding of land in idleness and penalizes land speculation. The tax encourages efficient land utilization ... it does not impede in any way the optimum use, or the optimum improvement, of the land.

James Carbray, National Council of Senior Citizens, Los Angeles: What we are doing by the present taxing policies of the city, county and state is creating slum areas at a faster degree by virtue of those taxing policies than we are eliminating them as a result of urban redevelopment.

Lawrence Weinberg, Beverly Hills homebuilder: Land in 1950 cost us $3,000 an acre. Today [13 years later] it is costing us $30,000 an acre. The finished lot back then represented 17.5 percent of the sales price. Today it represents 32 percent.

Elmer E. Botsai, Chairman, Building Code Committee, California council of the American Institute of Architects: [T]o support Mr Weinberg's statement [above] ... it is a commodity bought and sold on the open market. It fluctuates with the cost of land speculation and the causes of this property speculation include property taxes, advance zoning [zoning more land for higher use than market demands justify], and low taxation on unimproved property.

John W. Dyckman, Chairman, Center for Planning and Development Research, University of California-Berkeley: [L]eapfrogging of development over potential building sites into the more unspoiled countryside [reflects] the tendency of landowners in the near-in urban area to value their land at a very optimistic expectation of future price. They feel that their land's accessibility to the central city enhances its value compared with more remote holdings. As a result, developers who are aiming at lower-price developments will jump over the more expensive land in search of cheaper land.

Samuel E. Wood, Executive Director, California Tomorrow: Assessors throughout California are undervaluing land in relationship to improvements, contrary to the state constitution. In Orange and San Diego Counties vacant land is assessed about one-fifth the level at which homes are assessed. This land is then picked up by the speculator and developers are forced to skip over it and build urban islands beyond.

Chairman Douglas: *Mr Wood, [in your statement] you used a word which was unfamiliar to me. How would you define "slurb"?* *(Answer)* **Wood:** Alfred Heller and I invented that word when we were trying to describe the uncontrolled growth taking place in California. We combined urban and slum to get slurb. It simply stands for our sloppy, sleazy, slovenly sort of cities.

Allan Temko, Director, Study of Industrialized Environment, Twentieth Century Fund, urban historian: The chief physical fact of the West is that it is a desert. Water is common wealth – or should be common wealth. That was the spirit of the Reclamation Act of 1902, the greatest planning instrument we ever had. The state of California has circumvented that law – I believe illegally... When subsidized water is brought to parcels of 25,000 acres, this is an unconscionable enrichment of unearned increment for the large landowners.

Nathan Glazer, Sociology Professor, University of California: The major problem in the slums is not housing for the poor – it is income for the poor. We should look ahead to a time when the poor ... have enough money to fix housing up on their own.

William Sluis, reporter, Santa Barbara New Press: [In Santa Barbara] land was assessed at 22.5 percent of market value, improvements at 45 percent. There was simply no incentive to improve the structures to meet city code standards because each improvement was slapped with a 45 percent assessment. The split assessment ratio resulted in an incentive to keep existing shacks on the land.

Hans Schiller, Mill Valley, California, planning consultant: I advocate the development of a new land ethic. Land ownership at this point in history is largely a salacious concept, a futile concept hardly in keeping with democratic philosophy. Historically, it has been the large landholdings which have had the most retarding effect on the promulgation of human rights and social equity.

John C. Weaver, Program Director, Allegheny Roundtable: It is very common to hear people saying there is something wrong with a system that brings the assessors, as soon as a permit is issued for a building, even a small addition to a property, to "punish us for committing an improvement".

Leslie Carter, member, Neighborhood Youth Board No. 4, Manhattan: We want jobs. We have been unemployed for years, hundreds of years, and we are tired. So you can make all the plans you want. It will blow back in your face. You talk about slums. Do you know what creates slums? You know what slums is, and what creates it. You want to build. You must start building a person first. A person is more important than the house. We believe in the person first, economically, socially, physically and spiritually.

Leon Seidel, small business owner, Manhattan (referring to witnesses for cooperative housing): They completely forgot to tell you what happened to the people who live there, what happened to the businesses. They didn't tell you that the nonprofit United Housing Foundation has a wholly owned private corporation that is making a heck of a lot of money. These pious men have just come up here to give you a bunch of poppycock. They didn't tell you what happened to the 3,200 families dislocated, or the several hundred businesses that were dislocated.

Catherine Brooks, grassroots representative, the Bronx: I speak for a majority of the minority. We are not concerned about integrated housing. We are concerned about adequate housing. There is rats and roaches everywhere, and no reason why we have to pay the same taxes. There is no reason why our children have to be brought up under these conditions.

Franz Lichter, political party district leader, Manhattan: Housing Code enforcement [in New York City] under two administrations – Democratic and Republican – has been a complete failure. Before your Commission, leader after leader – very learned gentlemen – say, "What we have to do is really bring in private capital." I do hope we are not going to bribe the rich so we take care of the poor. I don't think the question of housing can be solved by taking care of our friends in Chase Manhattan. I think it's a problem of more government effort, more government spending.

Labron K. Shuman, council for Local 332, Philadelphia: We've got plenty of studies. I'll bet you could almost fill this room up with studies of North Philadelphia – the housing problems and all the other problems that go with it. But where's the action? That's the only thing that's going to cure what is a truly sick society.

Lee Datts, Jr, Philadelphia citizen: I represent the poor. We're not looking for you to do everything for us. We're looking to do something for ourselves. You can take this anti-poverty thing and drop it in the lake. You have only built up another lawyer, another minister. Until you get one of the poor out of the gutter and let him help his people, you have done nothing.

APPENDIX D

Starcke's Unique Sermon

VIGGO STARCKE, leader of Denmark's Justice Party and minister without portfolio of his country's cabinet, toured the United States. Speaking at the Unitarian Church in Columbus, Ohio, he gave a sermon entitled "Our Daily Bread". Using little buns or loaves of bread that he had in his pockets, Starcke creatively illustrated fundamental economics. The following brief extracts and summary give the essence of the sermon, although the good humor and deep philosophy of Starcke's talk are only found in the full text (published as a pamphlet by Land and Liberty, London).

When, after plowing the field, sowing the seed, harvesting the wheat, grinding the flour and baking the bread (he takes a tiny loaf from his pocket), a voice within you says, "*My bread is mine*," this is the beginning of **justice**.

If you are interested only in your own bread, that is **self-righteousness**.

If a voice within bids you to follow the Golden Rule so rights you enjoy apply to others, **righteousness** and **love** lead you to say (he takes out another loaf), "*Your bread is yours*."

If someone takes what you produced, saying, "*Your bread is mine*," that is **theft** and **injustice**. This is so even if the law permits it, as when others withhold the land and workplace you need unless you agree to give up to them some of the fruits of your labor (he breaks off chunks of both loafs, dropping them on the floor).

If a neighbor's harvest fails, or he becomes ill, and your heart leads you to say, "*My bread is yours*," that is **charity** (he takes out

227

another loaf and tosses it to a man in the front row). Starcke then talks of dangers, to both givers and receivers, if charity becomes a substitute for justice.

Using more loaves, he goes on to reveal in everyday terms critical aspects of social welfare, community, communism and equality. Noting that people hunger and thirst while the world produces more than we can eat or drink, he concludes:

The bread you produced is *yours*. The bread I produced is *mine*. But the prerequisite for every form of daily bread is that which none of us has produced – the riches of the earth and the powers of nature revealed in the value of land. It is *ours* and must belong to all of us.

APPENDIX E

A Property Tax Primer

FOLLOWING is a brief discussion of the basic aspects of the property tax.

The *conventional property tax*, also known as a real estate or *ad valorem* tax, is common throughout the United States and much of the world. It is based on two main components, the value of the *land* and the value of *improvements* on the land. These improvements are the man-made additions to the site such as a house, commercial building, factory, barn, orchard, hut, or skyscraper.

Conventional Property Tax

As shown in the graphic above, the assessed values of the land and improvement are added to show the *total value.* An assessor's job is to determine these two values for each lot or parcel in the city, county, township or other taxing jurisdiction. These total values are then multiplied by the jurisdiction's *property tax rate* to produce the *annual tax bill* owed by each property owner.

Under a *pure land tax*, as used in parts of New Zealand and elsewhere, only the socially created or naturally created land values are taxed, so there is no tax on the man-made improvement values.

Two-Rate Property Tax

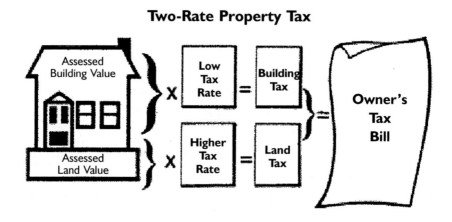

The *two-rate tax* pioneered in Pittsburgh, Pennsylvania has many names – graded tax, two-tier tax, split-rate tax, land value tax (LVT) and site value tax (SVT). As shown in the graphic above, each property's land value is multiplied by the jurisdiction's land tax rate to produce its *land tax bill*; each property's improvement value is multiplied by a lower improvement tax rate to produce its *improvement tax bill*; the sum of these two bills is the *total annual tax bill* owed by each parcel owner.

How are land and improvement values determined? The short answer is *the market*. A property's market price is what is agreed to by a willing buyer and a willing seller, neither being under unusual pressure or influence, as in the case of a trade or exchange with a family member.

Only a small portion of properties are sold annually, so appraisers (who perform valuations in the private sphere) and assessors (who perform valuations for public bodies) use a range of tools to assign values to land and buildings. These include comparisons with similar properties that do exchange hands, replacement costs of structures, capitalization of rents from income-producing properties, and so forth.

Some claim that the value of a site cannot be separated from the total value of the property. Yet commercial appraisers commonly arrive at these separate values to the satisfaction of their clients, who purchase or sell only the land and not the building, or vice versa. Assessors in places that tax land only, or that tax land and improvements at different rates, devise ways to distinguish their distinct values that are accepted as fair by citizens and businesses alike. It should be emphasized that expert assessing is essential to assure equitable treatment under any form of property tax, and that their professional job remains the same whether the conventional tax or the two-rate tax is being used.

How are property tax rates determined? A city or county, for instance, estimates its anticipated revenue from its other taxes and fees and aid from federal and state agencies for the coming budget year. It subtracts this total amount from its projected budget expenditures. The difference or shortfall typically is what it decides to raise from the property tax. Under the conventional system, the taxing jurisdiction divides this target figure – for example, $10 billion in a large metropolis – by the total property value in its borders – say $500 billion. This yields the necessary tax rate for the year – in this example, a 2 percent rate – which is then applied to each taxable property in the district.

In the case of a pure land tax, only the total land value in the jurisdiction – say $200 billion – would be used and the city-wide rate of 5 percent would be applied to each property owner's land value. Their homes or other improvements would be exempt from the tax.

In the case of a two-rate tax – sticking with the same example of $200 billion of land value and $300 billion of improvement value – local officials decide how much higher the rate should be on the land than on buildings. They may start with a modest differential in deference to political considerations, or a fairly high differential if a community is desperate to halt land speculation and spur wholesome growth.

Assessed values are often set at a fraction of market value, unwisely in my view, because they confuse taxpayers and hide inequities. A dollar of value should be a real dollar. If gas stations began calling half gallons a gallon, would we think the price of gas had been cut in half? Yet fractional assessments are not uncommon. Further complexities arise in jurisdictions that have a *classified property tax* – that is, with differing tax rates for residences, commercial properties, hotels, agriculture and the like. In extreme cases, this leads to owners of vacant lots in a huge metropolis trucking in one cow every day to win favorable farm tax rates. Even in less strange cases, classified taxes distort the market.

Finally, mention should be made of taxpayer appeals mechanisms. If properly operated, these become essential to preserve equity among taxpayers and to prevent errors, unintentional or otherwise, in the valuation of properties.

Index